BRITA
SEA MAM

Whales, dolphins, porpoises and seals, and where to find them

Jon Dunn, Robert Still and Hugh Harrop

WILD*Guides*

PRINCETON
press.princeton.edu

Published by Princeton University Press,
41 William Street, Princeton, New Jersey 08540
In the United Kingdom: Princeton University Press, 6 Oxford Street,
Woodstock, Oxfordshire OX20 1TW
nathist.press.princeton.edu

British Library Cataloging-in-Publication Data is available

Library of Congress Control Number 2012944344
ISBN 978-0-691-15660-6

Production and design by **WILD**Guides Ltd., Old Basing, Hampshire UK.
Printed in China

10 9 8 7 6 5 4 3 2 1

Contents

BRITAIN'S SEA MAMMALS

About this guide

This guide is divided into sections, each of which can either be used in isolation or in conjunction with another. There are sections covering the practicalities of how to look for marine mammals in order to optimise both the viewing experience and the chance of a successful identification (even after what may have been a brief encounter), and of course how to do so without causing disturbance to the animal in question. There are also sections examining the threats faced by, and the need for conservation of, our marine mammals and how you can get involved through recording and rescue.

The main sections of this book are the species and location guides. These aim to help you focus your searches for marine mammals according to your particular interest. There are specific site guides, and detailed and up-to-date distribution maps to help decide where to look. You may choose to design a trip to search for a certain species, or to visit a particular location or region in order to maximise your chances of seeing a range of different species. You might find yourself in a region with just a few hours of spare time – where can you go to stand a chance of seeing, say, Bottlenose Dolphins? This book aims to provide the answers.

The detailed species guides describe and illustrate the critical features of each species. With the advent of digital photography there is a better chance than ever before that even the most fleeting of marine mammal encounters may result in a record shot that can enable a definitive identification. This book not only provides the information needed to enable you to name the species you saw, but also provides hints on getting the most from your digital equipment so that you increase the chance of getting the best permanent record of your encounters.

Above all, it is hoped that this book will inspire people to get out and look for marine mammals around Britain. They are out there, though some are more easily seen than others. But part of the thrill and charm of an encounter with our marine wildlife is its unpredictability. Armed with this book, your chances of such an encounter will be increased and be all the more enjoyable.

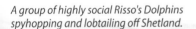

A group of highly social Risso's Dolphins spyhopping and lobtailing off Shetland.

The seas around Britain and Ireland

As an island sitting on the edge of the continental shelf, with the deep Atlantic Ocean to the west, the Arctic Ocean to the north, and warmer subtropical waters relatively close by, Britain is ideally placed both to host a rich resident marine mammal fauna and to be visited by species from much farther afield. It just needs time and effort to be put in to see them.

What makes British waters so good for marine mammals is the wide range of topography and oceanic conditions that give rise to distinct habitats that appeal to a broad range of species. In fact, approximately one third of the planet's cetacean species have been recorded here, and the coastline of the British Isles is home to internationally significant resident populations of two seal species.

Britain sits near to the edge of the European continental shelf, directly in the path of the North Atlantic Current. This northerly spur of the Gulf Stream brings warm water north-east across the Atlantic from the Americas and, as a result, the British

Major sea currents of Britain and Ireland

climate is milder and warmer than might be expected for its location. A second significant warm water current flows northwards up the continental shelf edge, bringing with it a planktonic community with origins in the Mediterranean.

The continental shelf itself runs from its eastern extremity in the Bay of Biscay, north-west past the Celtic Sea and the west coast of Ireland, then broadly north-east towards Norway, passing close to the west and north of Scotland. The continental shelf edge is a fabulously biodiverse area. Cold, nutrient-rich water driven by ocean floor currents hits the shelf slope and is forced upwards, eventually mixing with warmer water near the surface. The combination of nutrients and sunlight gives rise to an abundance of phytoplankton and zooplankton, which draws in plankton-feeding cephalopods and fish. Cetaceans are in turn drawn to these rich feeding areas. The relatively close proximity of the edge of the continental shelf to the coast of Britain and Ireland means that habitually deepwater species may be found close inshore on occasion.

The waters around Britain itself are generally shallow, less than 200 m deep on average. While many marine mammal species capitalise on the rich upwellings at the shelf edge, others favour these shallow waters, with some feeding in inshore waters close to land. Vantage points around the British coast provide opportunities to look for both cetaceans and pinnipeds. The seabed is not uniformly flat and even within the relatively shallow offshore waters there are channels, trenches of deeper water and seamounts that create considerable variations in sea depth. These features often create localised upwellings and hence richer feeding areas for cetaceans – areas such as in St George's Channel and the Irish Sea.

Away from the positively beneficial effects of both warm water currents and continental shelf upwellings there is a decrease in the diversity and abundance of marine life. As a consequence, the English Channel and the North Sea are both generally rather unproductive places in which to look for marine mammals. However there is an increase in cetacean and pinniped diversity as you move northwards through the North Sea that correlates with increasing water depth.

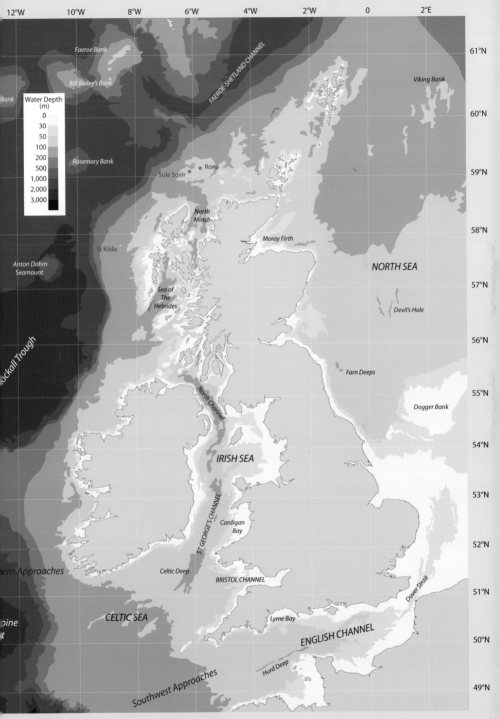

Water depths and features of the seas around Britain and Ireland

12°W 10°W 8°W 6°W 4°W 2°W 0 2°E

Faeroe Bank

Bill Bailey's Bank

FAEROE-SHETLAND CHANNEL

Viking Bank

61°N

60°N

Water Depth
(m)
0
30
50
100
200
500
1,000
2,000
3,000

Rosemary Bank

Sula Sgeir
Rona

59°N

North
Minch

Moray Firth

58°N

St Kilda

NORTH SEA

57°N

Anton Dohrn
Seamount

Sea of
The
Hebrides

Devil's Hole

56°N

Rockall Trough

North Channel

Farn Deeps

55°N

Dogger Bank

54°N

IRISH SEA

53°N

St GEORGE'S CHANNEL

Cardigan
Bay

52°N

ern Approaches

Celtic Deep

BRISTOL CHANNEL

Dover Strait

51°N

pine
t

CELTIC SEA

Lyme Bay

ENGLISH CHANNEL

50°N

Southwest Approaches

Hurd Deep

49°N

7

What is a marine mammal?

Marine mammals are not a distinct biological grouping, but are defined instead as mammals that have a reliance upon the marine environment for feeding – although not necessarily for breeding. Hence, cetaceans and pinnipeds are considered marine mammals – cetaceans being wholly dependent upon the marine environment throughout their life-cycle, and pinnipeds being dependent on the sea for food, but dry land for resting, moulting and breeding.

Britain is fortunate to have a burgeoning population of Eurasian Otter (*right*), which may be found in coastal habitats in parts of Britain and Ireland. Indeed, when Britain's rivers were widely polluted, the coastal areas provided some sanctuary for this beleaguered species. For the purposes of this book, the Eurasian Otter is not considered a true marine mammal as it is primarily a riverine species and is not strictly dependent upon the marine environment. Indeed, the otters that live in coastal areas of, for example, Shetland need to bathe in fresh water in order to rid themselves of sea salt that would otherwise reduce the insulative qualities of their fur.

Pinnipeds

All seals (and Walrus) belong to a subgroup of marine mammals called Pinnipedia, collectively known as pinnipeds. They are classified as part of the overarching order Carnivora, sharing common ancestors with, amongst others, bears and dogs – an interesting parallel given the shared curiosity Grey Seals and domestic dogs often show towards one another.

All pinnipeds share some fundamental characteristics and, while generally cumbersome and ungainly on land, are well adapted to a marine environment. The limbs have evolved into webbed flippers, and the body is streamlined for manoeuvrability underwater – even their reproductive organs are retractable into the main body mass to minimise drag when swimming. They also have a thick layer of blubber that provides insulation, and a circulatory system that redirects blood away from the body surface to minimise heat loss. Further adaptations are: nostrils that close when submerged; eyes with a protective clear membrane that allows excellent vision both above and below the water; and whiskers which, in conditions of low visibility, provide information about their surroundings. When diving, pinnipeds regulate the flow of blood to their organs, and are able to empty their lungs completely without ill-effect when diving deeply.

Pinnipeds are carnivorous and hunt by pursuing their prey. They feed on a wide variety of marine fish, cephalopods and molluscs, though they may feed opportunistically on seabirds and even other seals. Although most pinnipeds are generalist feeders, some species are specialists, such as the Ringed Seal that feeds almost exclusively on crustaceans.

Young pinnipeds are born on land, and are suckled by their mother for a period that ranges from just a few days to several weeks. The pups have a pelage (or coat) that is suited to the environment into which they have been born. For example, the pups of Arctic species are born with very fluffy, insulating coats that are moulted relatively quickly to the adult coat, after which the pup takes to the water. On the other hand, the pups of some species found in relatively warmer latitudes, such as the Common Seal, are born with coats that allow them to take to the water almost immediately.

Females give birth annually, though the time of year depends upon the species. The movements and occurrence of certain pods of Killer Whale are timed to coincide with the pupping season of some pinniped species.

There are approximately 35 species in the subgroup Pinnipedia, comprising three distinct families: the Otariidae; the Phocidae; and the Odobenidae.

The Otariidae, (known as eared or walking seals) are built for speed and maneuverability over short distances in water, using both their powerful hind and front flippers for propulsion. Their ears are external and their hind flippers can turn to point forwards, enabling them to walk (after a fashion) on all fours on dry land.

The Phocidae (known as earless seals) are built for economy of movement in water and have highly adapted hind flippers that are more 'tail' than limbs. This enables them to swim efficiently over great distances but somewhat hinders their movement when out of water. On land they use a combination of their front flippers and abdominal muscles to move, shuffling along like ungainly caterpillars on dry land – sliding along slightly more gracefully if the surface is slippery. In water they propel themselves through side-to side movements of their body and hind flippers and use their front flippers to steer.

The sole representative of the Odobenidae, the Walrus, displays a combination of features found in the other pinniped families inasmuch as it has hind flippers that turn and allow it to walk on dry land (like the Otariidae); and has internal ears (like the Phocidae).

Only Walrus, and some representatives of the Phocidae have occurred in Britain.

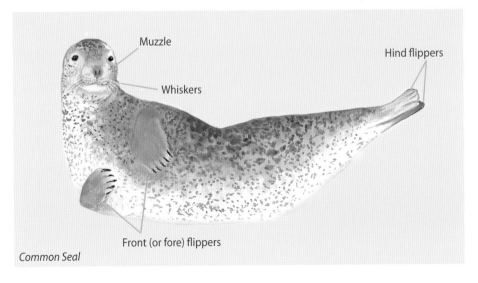

Common Seal

Cetaceans

Whales, dolphins and porpoises belong to an order of marine mammals called Cetacea, collectively known as cetaceans. Like terrestrial mammals, cetaceans are warm-blooded, breathe air into their lungs through their nostrils, and suckle their young. However, unlike all other mammals (except for the dugong and the manatees) cetaceans live exclusively in water.

Nature is a good designer, and cetaceans' adaptation to life in the marine environment has been so profound that many have evolved to resemble fish (sharks in particular) in both form and structure. The orientation of the tail should be noted when comparing sharks and cetaceans; in the former, the tail is orientated vertically, and in the latter the flukes are in a horizontal plane.

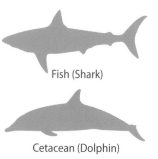

Fish (Shark)

Cetacean (Dolphin)

There are approximately 90 species within the Cetacea, comprising two suborders: the Mysticeti, or baleen whales; and the Odontoceti, or toothed whales.

Cetaceans come in all shapes and sizes and have evolved sufficiently to have adapted to all manner of aquatic habitats, and to be able to exploit a wide variety of food sources. They range from the deep-diving, squid-hunting Sperm Whale of the open ocean to fish- and shrimp-eating dolphins found in freshwater rivers; and from the huge 25 metre-long filter-feeding Blue Whale to the compact 1·5 metre-long fish-hunting Harbour Porpoise.

All cetaceans have the following features in common:
- they breathe air through blowholes situated on or near the top of the head;
- their ancestral front limbs have evolved to form flippers, and their hind limbs have vanished altogether to create an efficient hydrodynamic body shape;
- some or all of the neck vertebrae are fused (depending on the species) to stiffen their neck in order to enable high speed swimming;
- they have a greater tolerance to carbon dioxide, and lungs that are way more efficient at processing oxygen than any terrestrial mammal – essential for a mammal that must dive frequently, sometimes to extreme depths, to feed; and
- they have a layer of fat, known as blubber, beneath the skin to insulate them – rather than fur as in most other mammals.

The feeding techniques and strategies of different cetaceans are many and varied.

Baleen whales use a filter-feeding system that utilises plates of keratin edged with bristles. These plates are located along the upper jaw in a close arrangement. When a whale opens its mouth, water pours in and (in the rorquals) the ventral pleats expand to accommodate the water. The whale then pushes its tongue forward (and contracts its pleats) to force the water out through the baleen plates, the bristles trapping any prey inside the mouth.

Toothed whales, as the name suggests, have teeth on the upper and lower jaw – which is often elongated to form a distinct 'beak'. These species tend to be smaller than the baleen whales and hunt by pursuit. Many toothed whales find their prey in deep and dark or murky waters using echo-location. A high frequency click is produced by passing air through a special bony 'nostril' situated near the blowhole. This click is directed and magnified through a fatty organ located in the melon (the specially-shaped 'forehead' of the whale). Any returning echo is picked up by another fatty structure located in the lower jaw and is transmitted to the ear, enabling the animal to pinpoint its prey. Amazing!

Cetaceans give birth to live, fully formed young and, in common with terrestrial mammals, suckle their offspring. Many cetacean species are sociable animals, with complex family groups and social behaviours – both physical and vocal. Recent research has revealed that unique Humpback Whale songs that originated in a population off eastern Australia spread more than 10,000 km (6,000 miles) away over time and are now also sung by Humpback Whales in populations off French Polynesia. Many of the toothed cetaceans are aggressive towards one another and the scarred lines on the back and flanks of species such as Risso's Dolphin are a lasting reminder of these aggressive interactions.

The annual cycles of cetaceans are as variable as the many forms in which they are found: some species migrate great distances; others are relatively sedentary; some have short life-spans and reproduce relatively quickly; whereas others, like the Blue Whale, live a long time and reproduce very slowly indeed.

Baleen whales range in size from the Pygmy Right Whale, which barely reaches 7 m in length, to the massive Blue Whale, which grows to over 30 m. Instead of teeth, these whales have plates of baleen (whalebone) which hang from the upper jaw. These vertical plates can grow to over 2 m in length in some species and are used to filter enormous quantities of small fish and crustaceans. Baleen whales have two external nostrils or blowholes.

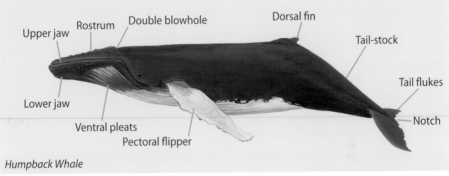

Humpback Whale

Toothed whales range in size from the huge Sperm Whale, with a maximum length of 18 m, to the diminutive Harbour Porpoise, which reaches a maximum length of 1·8 m. Besides having teeth, the Odontoceti are distinguished by having only one external nostril or blowhole. Nearly 70 species of toothed whale are recognised, the smallest of which are generally known as dolphins or porpoises.

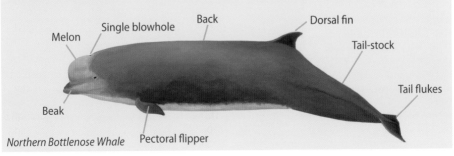

Northern Bottlenose Whale

Marine mammal families

Mysticeti – Baleen Whales

BALEEN WHALES

Families: Balaenidae and Balaenopteridae (Rorquals)

North Atlantic Right Whale
(*page 108*)

Minke Whale (*page 62*)
Fin Whale (*page 64*)
Humpback Whale (*page 66*)
Sei Whale (*page 92*)
Blue Whale (*page 109*)

With the exception of the
Minke Whale, all baleen

Fin Whale

whales that may be encountered in British waters are large to very large. They include the Blue Whale, the largest animal ever to have lived on Earth. Baleen whales do not possess teeth, instead having a series of comb-like structures called baleen plates that hang from the upper jaw. They feed by opening their cavernous jaws as they swim along; when the mouth is closed, water is strained through the baleen plates leaving quantities of small fish and zooplankton trapped inside. Most members of this group migrate long distances between their cold water summer feeding grounds and warm water winter breeding grounds. Despite their enormous size, baleen whales are streamlined and capable of considerable speed. They have large, flattened heads with a centrally located twin blowhole. The larger species can exhale a vertical blow several metres high. The sole representative in the region of the four species of Balaenidae is the extremely rare North Atlantic Right Whale, which differs from the rorquals in lacking a dorsal fin and having a distinctive 'V'-shaped blow. The eight species of Balaenopteridae (known as rorquals – from the Norwegian *røyrkval*), of which five have been recorded in British waters, are characterised by the expandable rows of pleated and grooved folds of skin running from the throat to the navel.

Odonticeti – Toothed Whales

SPERM WHALES

Families: Physeteridae and Kogidae

Sperm Whale (*page 94*)

Pygmy Sperm Whale (*page 110*)
Dwarf Sperm Whale (*page 111*)

Both families of sperm
whales are toothed whales
characterised by a bulky
body, a squarish head that
is large in proportion to
the body, and a narrow,

Sperm Whale

underslung lower jaw lined with teeth. The single blowhole is located slightly to the left of the top of the head producing a blow that is angled forward and to the left. All known species of sperm whale have been recorded in British waters. The Physeteridae comprises one species, the Sperm Whale, which is the largest toothed whale; the Kogidae comprises two species, which are among the smallest toothed whales. All sperm whales specialise in hunting deep-sea squid, and are therefore usually found far from land.

BEAKED WHALES **Family: Ziphiidae**

Northern Bottlenose Whale (*page 96*)
Cuvier's Beaked Whale (*page 98*)

Sowerby's Beaked Whale (*page 101*)
Gervais' Beaked Whale (*page 103*)
True's Beaked Whale (*page 102*)
Blainville's Beaked Whale (*page 102*)

Cuvier's Beaked Whale

Beaked whales are medium-sized whales with a distinctive protruding jaw, or beak. The forehead is often bulbous and houses the 'melon' used in echo-location. Their streamlined body profile, with the dorsal fin located two-thirds of the way along the back, is also distinctive. Due to their similar body shape and colouration, most beaked whales are notoriously difficult to identify – particularly the four species of the genus *Mesoplodon* (*pages 100–103*) that have been recorded in British waters. Very little is known about the identification and habits of this genus but the most reliable difference between them is the position of the protruding teeth that irrupt from the lower jaw of mature males. Females and immatures are seemingly almost impossible to identify at sea. Any observer will almost certainly have to note, and ideally photograph, the head and beak to have a chance of identification.

Six of the 21 known species of beaked whale have occurred in British waters. However, because of their deep-water habits and unobtrusive behaviour almost nothing is known about any of them. Beaked whales are capable of diving to great depths and for considerable periods of time in search of their squid and deep-sea fish prey.

BLACKFISH **Family: Delphinidae**

Long-finned Pilot Whale (*page 72*)
False Killer Whale (*page 114*)

Killer Whale or Orca (*page 68*)
Melon-headed Whale (*page 115*)

Blackfish include the largest members of the dolphin family. They are predominantly black in colour (hence the name), with a relatively large dorsal fin. The beak is either small or absent, and the jaw is rounded. Like other dolphins, blackfish are highly social, often spending their entire lives in a discrete family group. They are also very demonstrative and regularly spy-hop, tail-slap and breach. They are efficient, pack-hunting predators capable of considerable speed and feed on a wide variety of fish, squid and other sea life, including marine mammals. Of the six species of blackfish, only the Long-finned Pilot Whale and Killer Whale are seen regularly in British waters.

Long-finned Pilot Whale

DOLPHINS

Family: Delphinidae

Dolphins are considerably smaller than most whale species and have slim, streamlined bodies, usually with a prominent dorsal fin located centrally along the back. In most species the head tapers gently to a prominent beak containing many sharp teeth. The exception is Risso's Dolphin, which is blunt-headed and lacks a beak. Many dolphin species have body patterns and colours that are useful for identification. Dolphins are generally social animals, capable of great speed and spectacular acrobatics, and often occur in large groups. They feed on a wide variety of squid, fish and other marine life. Over 30 dolphin species occur worldwide, mainly in shelf waters, although some species inhabit the open sea and others can be found in freshwater rivers.

Short-beaked Common Dolphins

PORPOISES

Family: Phocoenidae

Porpoises are the smallest of all cetaceans at between 1·2–2·0m in length. They are relatively robust, though streamlined, and lack a prominent beak. Most species are timid and unobtrusive, rarely performing the acrobatics typical of some dolphins. Porpoises inhabit inshore waters where they feed predominantly on small fish. Unfortunately, many coastal populations have declined significantly as a result of the pressures of pollution, overfishing and accidental capture in fishing nets. Harbour Porpoise is the only representative of the family, that comprises six species, to occur in British waters.

Harbour Porpoise

SEALS Family: Phocidae

Grey Seal (*page 48*)
Common (or Harbour) Seal (*page 44*)
Ringed Seal (*page 54*)
Bearded Seal (*page 55*)
Harp Seal (*page 56*)
Hooded Seal (*page 57*)

The seals found in the North Atlantic and Arctic regions are all true, or earless, seals with, as the name suggests, no visible external ears. Designed for underwater efficiency, their hind flippers are used to great effect for propulsion when at sea. However, on land all Phocid seals are ungainly, using their bellies and front flippers to 'caterpillar' along. Like the cetaceans, a thick layer of blubber beneath the skin provides insulation, buoyancy and acts as an energy store. Their diet consists primarily of fish, but other marine species such as crustaceans (almost exclusively so in the case of Ringed Seal) and occasionally seabirds may be taken. Six of the18 Phocidae species have been recorded around the British coast.

WALRUS Family: Odobenidae

Walrus (*page 53*)

Walrus

Now exclusively an Arctic species, the Walrus is the sole surviving species of what was once a diverse and geographically widespread family. Walrus are long-lived, social animals unique amongst the pinnipeds for their prominent tusks. They feed almost exclusively on molluscs. Walrus have always played an important role in the culture of people who live in the Arctic but improved hunting techniques saw their population crash during the 19th and early 20th centuries. More recently the population has increased, though it remains fragmented and at a lower level than in historical times. The Walrus is a very rare vagrant to Britain.

Grey Seal

Observing marine mammals

Where to look

One of the joys, and at the same time frustrations, of cetacean watching is its unpredictability. Even though some species are resident year-round and others are migratory, and some species favour shallow inshore waters whilst others prefer deep waters beyond the coastal shelf, when it comes to cetacean watching nothing can be taken for granted – and nothing is impossible. Species can sometimes be found far from their favoured habitats – for example, the first confirmed British record of Dwarf Sperm Whale was in shallow inshore waters; a far cry from the deepwater habitat with which this squid-hunting whale is normally associated.

Most cetaceans occupy a position high up the food chain, and as such tend to occur in lower population densities than their prey. Furthermore, as all cetaceans spend much of their time out of human sight underwater, even those resident species of inshore waters can be frustratingly elusive. However, the patient and informed observer can take steps to shorten the odds of enjoying a cetacean sighting. Knowing where, when and how to look are all critical first steps.

Viewing from land, observers should seek headlands – particularly promontories that jut out a distance from the adjacent coast. Such vantage points offer both a better field of view for the observer than one at sea-level, and are often closer to deeper water than other points along the coast (see *How to look: from land, page 18*).

Putting yourself into the cetaceans' habitat should increase your chances, and may result in superlative views of marine mammals. There is a growing industry of boat operators offering wildlife-watching trips in inshore waters. Often such boat operators have a very good local knowledge of the habits of their local cetacean populations, and can help you get the views you seek.

Alternatively, commercial ferry operators offer a number of different advantages to the prospective whale-watcher; their vessels are much larger, are usually more stable than small inshore boats and offer a better vantage point from the higher elevation of their passenger decks. Moreover, many such ferries cross considerable distances at sea, and a voyage can transect a range of cetacean habitats, from inshore waters through deeper water and back inshore again. The most well-known of these are the routes to Spain from England that pass through the Bay of Biscay, from which a mouthwatering variety of cetaceans have been recorded, including rarely encountered and enigmatic *Mesoplodon* beaked whales (see *How to look: at sea, page 19*).

Seals represent less of a challenge since their habits are much more predictable and they are, in the main, very faithful to certain stretches of the coastline of Britain (see *Locations, pages 26–41*).

When to look

There is a golden rule for watching cetaceans – the more time you spend looking for them, the more likely you are to be lucky. There will be a lot of times when the sea appears empty – but when something suddenly breaches as if out of nowhere, all the time you have put in watching will seem worthwhile.

Some, though by no means all, of the cetacean species recorded to date in British waters are a little more predictable insofar as we know roughly when and where they should be around and about. For example, Harbour Porpoises may be found year-round in inshore waters and our ability to see them is limited only by the sea state. Cetaceans of course do not follow any set rules, so seeing them comes down to positioning yourself in a likely place, at the right time, and putting in the hours looking for them.

The greatest diversity of cetacean species occurs in British waters in summer and early autumn and, combined with the likelihood of better weather conditions, this represents the best time of year to look for them. At this time of year British waters are at their richest, as the longer hours of daylight and warming of the surface water combine to initiate an explosion of phytoplankton –

the most abundant foundation of the marine food chain. With this profusion of phytoplankton comes a corresponding surge in the abundance of zooplankton and fish, and hence cetaceans.

Other times of year should not be wholly discounted – calm weather at any time of year is worth taking advantage of, and some species like Long-finned Pilot Whale occur in British waters in the greatest numbers as they migrate past.

For the resident British seals, time of year is somewhat less critical – both Grey and Common Seal are present year-round and spend a proportion of each day hauled out. So timing becomes more dependent on the location in question and the behaviour you hope to see. Many seals allow themselves to be 'stranded' by the falling tide, so low tide often represents the best time of day to see seals on dry land.

Weather conditions in Britain are notoriously variable, depending upon both the time of year and, to an extent, the area of Britain in question. Winter months are generally dominated by successions of wet and windy weather fronts that track north-east from the Atlantic. These create disrupted sea conditions for long periods, in particular along those areas of coast or sea that are exposed to the prevailing wind.

With the onset of milder weather in the spring the weather improves and by the summer months drier, sunnier weather and calmer sea conditions may be expected. In late summer and early autumn these conditions can last for weeks at a time, and are thus a peak time for whale-watching. With the autumn equinox in September the weather becomes less predictable and more stormy, steadily deteriorating with the impending winter. Various weather conditions can hinder the observer's ability to find cetaceans – fog; rain; and even the glare of the sun can reduce visibility.

The effect of the wind on the sea (the size and nature of the waves and swell) is known as the sea state and is by some margin the most important determining factor in the ability to locate cetaceans where they are present. Sea state is described on a scale of 1–9 in the World Meteorological Organisation code (see *below*). Clearly, the calmer the sea state the better the observer's chances of spotting cetaceans breaking the surface – anything over sea state 3 and there is a far greater possibility that wave troughs or the visual 'noise' of a disturbed sea will reduce the chances of any signs of cetaceans, such as blows or dorsal fins, being noticed.

Mirror calm; whale-watching heaven!

Slight ripples; no white water

Small wavelets; glassy crests, no white caps

Large wavelets; crests begin to break; few white caps

Longer waves; many white caps; whale-watching becomes more tricky

Moderate waves of longer form; some spray

Large waves; many white caps; frequent spray

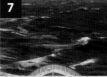
Sea heaps up; white foam blows in streaks

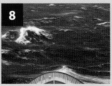
Long, high waves; edges breaking; foam blows in streaks

High waves; sea begins to roll; dense foam streaks; scary!

Watching Britain's sea mammals

On land

- Pick a suitable vantage point – reasonably high in order to maximise your field of view, and if possible extending some way out into the sea – headlands are ideal.

- Prepare to be patient – you may well be looking for cetaceans for some hours; so make the duration as comfortable as you reasonably can. Consider taking a small folding camping stool; food and drink; weather-appropriate warm and/or wind and waterproof clothing (remember, you can always shed layers, gloves and hat if needs be, but they are of no use to you if left at home); sun-block; antihistamines *etc.*

- Use the right optics – 8× or 10× magnification binoculars provide a wide field of view and are a significant improvement over the naked eye; any higher magnification binocular is likely to be unwieldy and of poorer optical quality. A spotting telescope with 30× magnification mounted on a tripod will greatly increase your chances of picking out distant animals. It may be helpful if your telescope's eyepiece is a zoom, as these can provide up to 60× magnification in an instant.

- Keep looking – scan the sea with your binoculars, and use your telescope if you have one to get better views of animals once you have found them. The wider field of view of binoculars enables you to search a greater area of sea more easily; and you won't miss that Minke Whale that is feeding close inshore while you're scanning the far horizon!

- Record your sightings – have a notebook and a pen with you; if you don't have a digital camera to hand to obtain a record shot of a sighting, it's still important to record any details noted (numbers, behaviour, appearance *etc.*) at the time. These data may be of use subsequently.

At sea

- As on land, try to get a good vantage point – high and with a good field of view ahead of the vessel. Dress warmly – it is often much cooler at sea than it is on land. Be prepared for the effects of the sun – cover up, use sun-block, and wear a hat.

- Seasickness is no fun at all – try to avoid it by remaining hydrated and with a full stomach – take water and plain food snacks with you. If you begin to feel nauseous, fresh air and concentrating on the far horizon may help. And remember, there's no shame in taking motion-sickness medication – many people who work at sea do so regularly, after all. Take advice from your pharmacist, and remember that these medications may make you feel drowsy.

- In the main, binoculars are the best optical aid to use at sea – if the vessel is sufficiently large and stable, a spotting telescope on a tripod may still be useful. Attach soft, foam rubber pads (sections of pipe lagging are good for this) to the feet of the tripod to absorb some of the vibration from the ship's engines.

- Have your camera charged and ready – you have a far higher chance of a close encounter with cetaceans at sea than when looking from land.

Photography

- For best results use a digital SLR with an interchangeable zoom lens. A focal length of 70–200 mm or 100–400 mm is ideal. Always attach a strap to the camera or lens and wear it around your neck.

- For fast moving subjects (e.g. dolphins) set the shutter speed as high as possible. Usually a minimum shutter speed of 1/2,000th sec. is required for 'freezing the action' and getting sharp images. To get the maximum shutter speed, shoot with the lowest aperture possible or increase the ISO. When using a high ISO ensure your camera can handle 'noise-free' images. Most modern DSLRs allow people to shoot around ISO 800 with 'noiseless' results. Shooting is possible at ISO 3200 on top-of-the-range models.

- As whales and dolphins (and you, if you are on a boat!) are likely to always be moving, always use the focus-tracking mode if your camera has it.

- Try to use large memory cards (e.g. 16 Gb) – there is nothing worse than running out of memory and having to delete images to make room on a card in the middle of some action! Always carry spare memory cards.

- Charge your camera batteries before you head out and if possible always carry spares.

- Where possible, shoot in RAW mode – if not, choose the highest quality JPEG setting for the highest resolution.

- Make sure to check images using your histogram when you are in the field so you can make adjustments as you go. Take a couple of test shots of the sky or people around you to make sure everything is set correctly before you see any animals.

- Keep your lens clean! Salt spray is not good for cameras or lenses so try and keep your gear dry by using lens hoods and custom made lens / camera covers. A UV filter will protect the front lens element and a simple plastic bag secured with elastic bands is a simple solution for covering your gear. NEVER polish a lens that has sea spray on it – the salt might scratch the glass and damage it permanently.

Watching Britain's sea mammals

An encounter with cetaceans may, if you are fortunate, be a relatively prolonged experience affording plenty of opportunities to observe identification features and behaviour and secure a confident identification of the animals in question. The reality is sometimes rather different – whales and dolphins are unpredictable and may dive for long periods of time, during which they may move a considerable distance from where they were last seen. It may well be that an encounter will be brief and fleeting, and for this reason the cetacean-watcher should be prepared. It is all too easy in the excitement of the initial moment of discovery to not remain calm and observant – and then the encounter is over, and the opportunity to identify the animal gone with it. Photographs can help greatly as they may freeze details that may otherwise be overlooked (see *page 19*). The following general features should always be looked for, and a combination of these with any behaviour that is noted may help to secure an identification.

Size – may be difficult to judge, as there is often a lack of other features nearby that can provide scale, and distance may also prove deceptive. Where possible, if there are any nearby features – boats, seabirds, buoys *etc.* – these should be used to help provide some measure of scale. Bear in mind that typically only a small part of a cetacean's body will be visible above the surface of the water at any one time, and that different species may show more of themselves than others. So what you actually see is not necessarily a reliable indicator of the size of the animal in question.

Comparing a cetacean with an object of known size, such as a boat or seabird, can help in the estimation of size. In the photo (left) a boatload of people enjoy a simultaneous encounter with a White-beaked Dolphin and a Humpback Whale.

Shape – while all have a similar basic 'design', the variability in shape between the different species that may be encountered in British waters is considerable, even within families. For example, Risso's and Bottlenose Dolphins are, broadly speaking, grey dolphins, but note the steeply sloping forehead and straight back of Risso's Dolphin (*left*) compared with the more rounded forehead and slightly more rounded back of Bottlenose Dolphin (*right*).

Colouration – while some cetaceans have very distinctive colourations and patterns on their skin, actually seeing these features can be challenging – and colours and patterns may alter or be less visible depending on the light and viewing conditions. In the same way that the sea's colour may change from bright blue to leaden grey depending on the amount of sunlight and the sun's position in the sky, so too can the observer's perception of the colour of a cetacean. It may be that all you are able to say is that an animal looked light or dark; but even this may help in conjunction with other features observed at the time.

Bottlenose Dolphins are grey, but in evening light they can appear brown.

Dorsal fin – with the exception of the very rare Narwhal, Beluga and North Atlantic Right Whale, all British cetaceans have dorsal fins. The general shape and location of the dorsal fin varies between species and the differences are very useful for identification, particularly in the whales. Try to note the the shape of the fin itself; the size of the fin in relation to the body; and how far along the back the fin is located. For large whales it is helpful to note, if possible, where and when the dorsal fin appears relative to the whale's blowhole.

Variation in dorsal fin shape and location
TOP TO BOTTOM: *Minke Whale, Sowerby's Beaked Whale, Long-finned Pilot Whale and Short-beaked Common Dolphin.*

Blow – larger cetaceans often have a distinctive blow when they surface. The blow is a plume of moisture-laden air expelled as the animal surfaces and exhales. This varies between species in size, shape and orientation. Some species have single blowholes, others have double blowholes, some are straight on the head, but others (*e.g.* Sperm Whale) are offset resulting in an angled (instead of straight up) blow. In perfect viewing conditions these blows can help to identify an animal; however, blows are very variable depending upon circumstances and should be used with caution for identification purposes. Younger animals may have smaller blows than adults; the size of the blow may be bigger if the animal is surfacing after a long dive as opposed to when it is making shallow dives just below the surface; and, being vaporous, a blow's shape is easily altered by the wind.

A distant Fin Whale blows on surfacing – in calm conditions some blows can be seen over 5 km away.

Care should be taken to eliminate large, surface feeding fish – Basking Sharks are encountered in British waters during the prime summer/autumn cetacean-watching season, and may be a trap for the unwary.

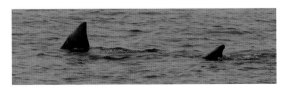

Watching Britain's sea mammals

Cetacean behaviour varies greatly between species and the circumstances of the encounter. Some behaviours may assist in identification – for example, some large whales regularly fluke as they dive, whilst others do not. Hence a whale observed doing this is more likely to be a Blue, Humpback or Sperm Whale rather than a Fin, Minke or Sei Whale. Like blows, many of these behaviours may not themselves be diagnostic of a species; but they can help in identification alongside other features that are noted.

Bow-riding – is the activity of cetaceans swimming in the pressure wave created ahead of larger objects moving through the water. Although usually observed around ships, this behaviour may also be seen around travelling large whales! It is typically exhibited by smaller cetaceans such as dolphins, and may provide observers with superlative views of the animals.

Porpoising – is when a cetacean leaps clear of the water while travelling at speed and re-enters the water headfirst. Often repeated, it is commonly associated with members of the dolphin family, such as these *Short-beaked Common Dolphins*.

Blowing (see also *page 21*) – is the term used when a plume of moisture-laden air is shot into the air as the animal surfaces and exhales. With larger whales, such as this *Fin Whale,* blows may be seen from some distance away in good viewing conditions.

Fluking – is a behaviour often associated with some of the larger whales, such as this *Humpback Whale,* when the animal raises its tail flukes vertically into the air as it dives.

Breaching – is the term used when an animal has propelled itself upwards so that most or even all of its body clears the water's surface – such as shown by this *Minke Whale*.

Lunge-feeding – is a feeding behaviour most commonly seen in baleen whales, such as this *Sei Whale*, when the animal rises vertically and at great speed with its mouth wide open in order to capture a large mouthful of prey items.

Lobtailing – is the term used when a large whale, such as this *Humpback Whale*, lifts its tail clear of the water and then slaps the flukes against the water's surface.

Tail-slapping – small cetaceans such as these *Risso's Dolphins* are capable of raising their tail flukes above the surface and then vigorously slapping them against the water, sometimes repeatedly.

Chorus line – is the activity, most often seen in the blackfish and dolphin families, when a group of animals, such as these *Risso's Dolphins*, surface simultaneously line-abreast.

Logging – is when cetaceans, such as these *Long-finned Pilot Whales*, rest motionless on the surface of the water, their bodies held horizontally.

Spy-hopping – is the behaviour in which the animal raises its head vertically from the water allowing it to see the immediate environs above the surface. Spy-hopping animals, such as these *Long-finned Pilot Whales*, usually sink smoothly back beneath the surface.

Where to watch Britain's sea mammals

The coastline of Britain and Ireland extends to over 26,000 km (16,000 miles) and supports a wide variety of marine habitats. The potential for those looking for cetaceans or pinnipeds is, therefore, vast and the aim of this section of the book is to highlight those locations that have a proven track record for sea mammal sightings. It is not intended to be comprehensive, definitive or prescriptive since there are many other sites that are worth visiting – and there is nothing to stop pioneers from seeking out new sites.

Keeping abreast of the latest sightings in a given region is essential if you are to get the most out of a sea mammal-watching trip. While our two resident seal species tend to be reasonably predictable in their habits and haunts, cetaceans and the rarer, vagrant seals are rather more unpredictable in their movements. Fortunately, interest in marine mammals is such that their sightings attract considerable public attention, and records can often be found online, sometimes within minutes of the initial sighting.

Sea Watch Foundation (SWF) operate a recent sightings collation service, whereby observers can submit details of any cetaceans they have seen in British waters. All the latest sightings are compiled by region and are available to view online (www.seawatchfoundation.org.uk). SWF also have a network of regional coordinators who can be contacted by visitors to their respective regions. Many areas have local grapevines that operate to disseminate breaking news as it happens, so providing your contact details to the regional coordinator in return for details of all sightings made on your trip may prove a fruitful exchange if something unusual turns up during your time in the area. Sightings of rare pinnipeds are often reported on the British Marine Life Study Society website (www.glaucus.org.uk). For all marine mammal sightings, it is also worth checking the frequently updated Mammals & Sealife pages of Birdforum (www.birdforum.net).

Care should be taken when choosing a trip operator for at-sea observation of marine mammals. Good operators will have an in-depth knowledge of their local marine fauna and will always put wildlife's best interests first, behaving in a responsible and sustainable manner that avoids causing disturbance (see *page 121*). There are a number of regional and national accreditation schemes designed to provide commercial wildlife tourism boat operators with the necessary guidelines and training to show their guests the marine wildlife in their area in a sensitive way. These schemes also enable visitors to choose with some confidence which boat operator to use. Nationally, the WiSe (Wildlife Safe) Scheme is designed to provide this peace of mind (www.wisescheme.org) and Planet Whale (www.planetwhale.com) provides a forum for customer reviews of operators.

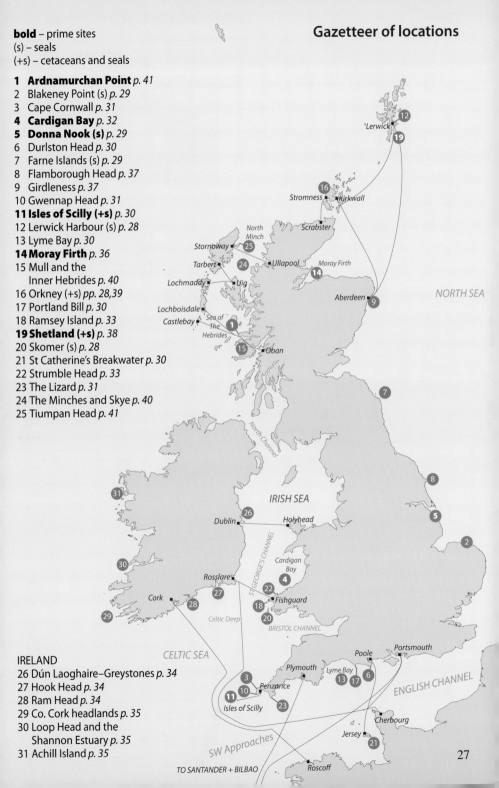

Gazetteer of locations

27

Locations: Seals

While both Grey and Common Seals may be encountered around much of the British coast, both species' propensity for using the same sites year-on-year for hauling out and pupping make them satisfyingly predictable animals to encounter in the wild. While by no means an exhaustive selection, the following sites have been chosen for their reliability, the quality of the viewing experience for the observer, and of course the lack of disturbance caused to the seals by our being there.

Skomer, Pembrokeshire, SW Wales
Grid ref: SM 760091 (Martin's Haven)
Nearest train station: Haverfordwest
(14 miles to Martin's Haven)

West Wales is home to a population of around 5,000 Grey Seals, and they can be seen readily year-round on the island of Skomer. Particular sites to check here are Pigstone Bay on the far western side; and at the Garland Stone, where their haul-outs on the low rocks exposed by the falling tide on the eastern side can be viewed from the clifftop opposite.

Skomer can be accessed by boat from Martin's Haven on the Welsh mainland, 2 miles from Marloes village. Note there is a landing fee payable on Skomer.

COMMERCIAL OPERATORS
www.pembrokeshireislands.co.uk

Lerwick harbour, Shetland
Grid ref: HU 477414 (Victoria Pier car park)

Shetland is home to both Grey and Common Seals, and they may be encountered almost anywhere around the archipelago's coastline. Lerwick harbour, however, offers a unique opportunity to get close to both species from the water; and being a commercial harbour with regular human activity, the seals of both species and in particular Grey Seals have become extremely tolerant of boat traffic and humans alike. Boat trips to see the seals and other marine wildlife leave from the Victoria Pier twice daily (see photo on *page 120*).

COMMERCIAL OPERATORS
www.seabirds-and-seals.com
www.shetlandwildlife.co.uk

Orkney
Like Shetland, Orkney hosts a large number of both Grey and Common Seals, and they may be encountered almost anywhere around the coastline.
The island of Stronsay hosts a high density of Grey Seals, especially in November and December when large rookeries form during pupping.

Donna Nook, Lincolnshire
Grid ref: TF 422998 (Stonebridge entrance)
Nearest train station: Cleethorpes (18 miles)

This Lincolnshire Wildlife Trust reserve comprises a complex of dunes, slacks and intertidal areas, with the predominant habitat being sandflats and raised sandbars. These provide haul-outs for both Grey and Common Seals. The reserve is most notable for the colony of breeding Grey Seals, one of the largest in Britain, and provides exceptional views from an organised area when the mothers pup in November and December. Visitors should park and enter the reserve via the Stonebridge entrance car-park only.

The Farne Islands, Northumberland
Grid ref: NU 219322
(Seahouses harbour car park)
Nearest train station: Chathill (4 miles)

The Farnes are accessible by boat from Seahouses harbour and their rocky shores are home to Grey Seals (the islands are also an excellent birdwatching destination in their own right). Boat trips vary in duration and destination, with some trips having more emphasis on seal-watching than others – so care should be taken when booking. (When landing on any of the islands, a landing fee will be payable to the National Trust.)

COMMERCIAL OPERATORS
www.farne-islands.com
www.farneislandsboattrips.co.uk
www.farneislandstours.co.uk

Blakeney Point, Norfolk
Grid ref: TG 007442 (Morston Quay car park)
Nearest train station: Sheringham (8 miles)

Both Grey and Common Seals breed and may be found on the sandbanks at the far end of Blakeney Point. The best views will be had by taking one of the local boat trips out to see the seals from the water.

Visitors should park at Morston Quay pay & display car park, and take a boat trip out to see the seals on their haul-outs. (The alternative, parking at Cley and walking out onto Blakeney Point is not recommended – this is a long way, extremely arduous, and will result in far more distant views of the seals.)

COMMERCIAL OPERATORS
www.beansboattrips.co.uk
www.sealtrips.co.uk

South West England is effectively a large peninsula protruding into the Atlantic. It should therefore come as no surprise that with close proximity to deep water comes a wide variety of cetacean species. Since 1980, 17 species have been recorded in the Southwest Approaches, and 14 from or near the English Channel coast. Of these, seven are either present year-round or recorded annually. In the region as a whole, cetacean species diversity declines moving east through the English Channel.

Isles of Scilly

Proximity to the Southwest Approaches makes Scilly a good stepping stone for at-sea sightings of cetaceans, either from the Scillonian ferry that regularly links the islands to the Cornish mainland, or from the small boats that make excursions out beyond the footprint of the archipelago in the summer months (see operators *opposite*). Species regularly seen in the summer are Short-beaked Common Dolphin and Harbour Porpoise, with Bottlenose and Risso's Dolphins seen more sporadically; however, almost anything is possible in this region, in particular the closer you get to the shelf edge. Deepwater species like Fin Whale, migratory species like Long-finned Pilot Whale, or warm water species like Striped Dolphin are all possibilities.

St Catherine's Breakwater, Jersey

Jersey's resident pod of Bottlenose Dolphins pass this breakwater daily on their way to feed in Bouley Bay and Fliquet Bay. Park in St Catherine's and walk to the end of the breakwater to observe – the peak feeding time for the dolphins is during the hours either side of high tide.

DORSET

Portland Bill, Dorset

Grid ref: SY 677685 (car park)
Nearest train station: Weymouth (9 miles)

Harbour Porpoise and Bottlenose Dolphin are a possibility here, with more offshore species (Short-beaked Common Dolphin and Long-finned Pilot Whale) also possible due to the location's projection into the English Channel. Park at the large car park at the end of the road, and view the sea from the low clifftop near the lighthouse.

Lyme Bay, Dorset

Grid ref: SY 463904 (West Bay car park) / SY 337916 (Lyme Regis car park)
Nearest train station: Axminster (14 miles West Bay / 6 miles Lyme Regis)

The deep waters of Lyme Bay provide regular records of Harbour Porpoise, White-beaked and Bottlenose Dolphins in the summer months. Less frequently recorded species include Short-beaked Common and Risso's Dolphins, and Long-finned Pilot and Minke Whales. Boat trips are the best way to obtain good views – either on organised cetacean-watching day-trips or private charters departing from West Bay or Lyme Regis.

Durlston Head, Dorset

Grid ref: SZ 032773 (Visitor car park)
Nearest train station: Wareham (11 miles)

Bottlenose Dolphins are seen periodically in Durlston Bay, apparently feeding around the reefs of Durlston Head, Peveril Point and Anvil Point. The best months for seeing them are April–May and October–November – less so in the summer months, possibly in response to the more intensive human activity in the bay at this time. There is ample pay & display car parking at the Durlston Country Park visitor centre, and from here it is a short walk to Durlston Head itself.

THE CORNISH HEADLANDS

Cape Cornwall, Cornwall

Grid ref: SW 351318
Nearest train station: Penzance (8 miles)

Four miles north of Land's End, near the small town of St Just, Cape Cornwall is probably the best location on the British mainland from which to look for Risso's Dolphin – they are reported sporadically from this location year-round. Harbour Porpoise is also present, as are Grey Seals. Park where the road to Cape Cornwall from St Just ends, and walk to the Cape itself.

Cape Cornwall

Gwennap Head, Cornwall

Grid ref: SW 371218 (Porthgwarra car park)
Nearest train station: Penzance (9 miles)

In the summer and autumn there are regular sightings of Harbour Porpoise and Minke Whale foraging in the tide-race around the edges of the Runnelstone Reef. Short-beaked Common Dolphin are reported regularly; Bottlenose and Risso's Dolphins more sporadically. Park at the small pay & display car park in Porthgwarra, and walk to the headland. (Note, Grey Seals are also often seen here.) There are regular wildlife-watching boat trips along this coastline that operate out of Penzance.

The Lizard, Cornwall

Grid ref: SW 703126 (The Lizard village)
Nearest train station: Falmouth (16 miles)

The Lizard is the most southerly headland of mainland Britain, and hence Lizard Point is a good location from which to look for a wide variety of cetaceans – in particular Short-beaked Common Dolphin and Harbour Porpoise, which are both seen regularly. There are also occasional sightings of Risso's and Bottlenose Dolphins, and Killer and Minke Whales. Parking is very limited at Lizard Point, so it is best to park in Lizard village and walk down Lighthouse Road to the Point.

Whale-watching by boat

Operator 'hotspots' are the Isles of Scilly, Penzance and Lyme Bay.

THE ISLES OF SCILLY
www.islandseasafaris.co.uk
www.scillyboating.co.uk
www.scillypelagics.com

CORNWALL
www.marinediscovery.co.uk

LYME BAY
www.naturetrek.co.uk

Ferry routes

There are a number of commercial ferry operators plying routes either within or emanating from the South West region. These boats, while not specifically cetacean-watching trips, provide stable viewing platforms through potentially rewarding waters: whether domestic, *i.e.* between the British mainland and the Isles of Scilly or the Channel Islands; or further afield, *i.e.* ferries that pass through the cetacean hotspot of the Bay of Biscay *en route* to northern Spain.

TO THE ISLES OF SCILLY
www.islesofscilly-travel.co.uk

TO JERSEY
www.condorferries.co.uk

TO SANTANDER AND BILBAO
www.brittany-ferries.co.uk

Looking west towards Samson from Porthloo Beach, St. Mary's, Isles of Scilly

The waters around Wales have had a relatively small range of cetacean species recorded in them, but are notable for the regularity with which eight species in particular are recorded, either as residents or annual visitors. Harbour Porpoise, Short-beaked Common and Bottlenose Dolphins are all present year-round in the region.

Long-finned Pilot Whale – fairly common, most sightings offshore in the middle of the Irish Sea; year-round but peaking in August–December.

Killer Whale – uncommon, primarily off the Dyfed coast; April–September.

Risso's Dolphin – uncommon, mostly in inshore waters around the Pembrokeshire islands, and the western end of the Lleyn Peninsula; April–September.

Minke Whale – fairly common in the central Irish Sea south to St George's Channel; most sightings May–October.

Fin Whale – uncommon, most sightings in St George's Channel; west of Ramsey Island and near the Smalls; June–October.

Cardigan Bay, Ceredigion

Cardigan Bay is one of the premier sites in Britain to see Bottlenose Dolphins from the shore – the resident Welsh population is estimated to number between 200 and 300 animals, and may be the source of animals seen in South West England.

New Quay is a particularly good location to look for them as they regularly swim close inshore and may be seen from the quayside. However, sightings are possible from almost any point along the coastline, and boat trips may provide spectacular encounters; other notable sites are Mwnt Beach (SN 195519) and Gwbert (SN 162499).

Also present in Cardigan Bay and visible from dry land as well as from boats are good numbers of Harbour Porpoise, with numbers peaking August–November.

Whale-watching by boat

There are a number of commercial operators based in Aberaeron, Cardigan, Haverfordwest and New Quay.

www.baytoremember.co.uk
www.dolphinsurveyboattrips.co.uk
www.newquayboattrips.co.uk
www.ramseyisland.co.uk
www.seamor.org
www.thousandislands.co.uk

Ferry routes

There are ferry crossings over the Irish Sea from both Fishguard (to Rosslare) and Holyhead (to Dun Laoghaire and Dublin). These are relatively short crossings of just a few hours, but provide an opportunity to look for cetaceans in deeper water.

www.irishferries.com
www.stenaline.co.uk

Ramsey Island, Pembrokeshire
Grid ref: SM 725252 (St Justinian's car park)
Nearest train stations: Fishguard (15 miles) &
Haverfordwest (16 miles)

The waters in the vicinity of Ramsey Island
and out to the edges of the Celtic Deep are a
particularly reliable site for boat-based sightings
of Short-beaked Common Dolphin and Harbour
Porpoise (and the island itself is a magnificent site
for Grey Seals). Minke Whale is also seen regularly
– for Short-beaked Common Dolphin and Minke Whale, the best time is July–September.
Boats depart from the St Justinian's Lifeboat Station, located 2 miles from St David's.

Strumble Head, Pembrokeshire
Grid ref: SM 895412 (car park)
Nearest train station: Fishguard (5 miles)

Strumble Head is notable primarily for sightings
of Harbour Porpoise – the species is regular here,
best seen on calm days when animals can be
spotted feeding amongst the tidal races between
the headland and the offshore Strumble Bank.
(Grey Seals also present in the general vicinity.)
Follow the minor road signposted to Strumble
Head from Fishguard to the car park at the end.

The coastline from New Quay to Tresaith has been established as a Marine Heritage Coast, a
voluntary community initiative aimed at conserving the area's rich marine wildlife including
Bottlenose Dolphin. This voluntary initiative was the first of its kind in Britain. An area 12
miles offshore and 24 miles up and down the coast has been designated a Special Area of
Conservation by the European Union, also in recognition of the rich marine life found here.

The excellent opportunities afforded by Ireland to anyone with an interest in seeing cetaceans should not be unerestimated. Irish waters are every bit as good as British waters and 24 species, from the diminutive Harbour Porpoise to the largest baleen whales, have been recorded to date. As in Britain, the diversity and range of species increases dramatically with proximity to the shelf edge, and headland and island sites along the spectacularly fractured south and west coasts of Ireland are particularly productive.

Cetacean diversity declines markedly off the north and east of the Irish landmass – although further south in the Irish Sea and close to St George's Channel a greater variety of species is recorded. The sites listed here are by no means an exclusive list – the wide range of suitable vantage points around Ireland mean that almost anywhere, in the right conditions, may prove fruitful. All sightings should be reported to the Irish Whale and Dolphin Group (IWDG) – www.iwdg.ie – which provides regular online updates of sightings from all around Ireland.

Dún Laoghaire–Greystones
This stretch of Dublin/Wicklow coast has, in recent years, become home to a small resident pod of Bottlenose Dolphins. They rarely appear to travel north of Dalkey Island, or south of Wicklow town, providing observers with a manageable 20 mile stretch of coast along which to search for them. The DART train that runs between Dún Laoghaire and Greystones provides a convenient platform from which to look. Harbour Porpoise and Risso's Dolphins are also recorded in the area.

Hook Head, Co. Wexford
A good number of cetacean species are attracted to the waters off Hook Head in the late winter every year, drawn by the abundance of spawning herring. Fin, Minke and occasional Humpback Whales; Short-beaked Common Dolphin and Harbour Porpoise have all been recorded in recent winters. Hook Head, unusually amongst cetacean-watching locations, provides particularly luxurious facilities for visitors at the Hook lighthouse – most notably boasting a café that provides a welcome temporary sanctuary during inclement weather.

Ram Head, Ardmore, Co. Waterford
Similar to Hook Head, Ram Head proves attractive to a range of cetaceans every winter by virtue of the inshore herring activity at this time of year. Fin Whales and Short-beaked Common Dolphins are particularly notable, often in proximity to fishing boats working in the area, and Harbour Porpoise are also present.

Loop Head, Co. Clare

County Cork headlands

Co. Cork has a succession of headlands and islands along the coast that provide ideal vantage points from which to look for cetaceans. From east to west: Old Head of Kinsale; Galley Head; Toe Head; Cape Clear Island; Mizen Head; Sheeps Head; and Dursey Island all afford excellent potential for land-based observations of a wide range of species, including Harbour Porpoise; Bottlenose, Short-beaked Common and Risso's Dolphins; and Fin, Humpback, Killer and Minke Whales.

Loop Head & Shannon Estuary, Co. Clare

Loop Head is but one of many headlands on the west coast of Ireland, and is notable for Minke Whale sightings in the autumn, peaking in September–October when they come close inshore. Other cetaceans regularly seen include Common and Bottlenose Dolphin and Harbour Porpoise, with Fin and Humpback Whales also recorded. The mouth of the Shannon is home to a population of 100+ Bottlenose Dolphins, and these may be best seen on one of the various local boat trips operating in the area.

Achill Island, Co. Mayo

Achill Head represents the considerable opportunity that much of Ireland offers the cetacean watcher away from the well-covered south and south-west coasts. The north-west of Ireland is relatively under-watched, and yet with proximity to the open Atlantic there is much potential beyond the usual quartet of Harbour Porpoise, Common and Risso's Dolphins, and Minke Whale.

Whale-watching at Dunree, Co. Donegal

Whale-watching by boat

There are a number of commercial operators venturing into the Irish Atlantic and in the Shannon Estuary.

CO. CORK
www.charterangling.ie
www.whalewatchwestcork.com
www.whalewatchwithcolinbarnes.com

CO. CLARE
www.dolphinwatch.ie
www.discoverdolphins.ie

Ferry routes

There are a number of commercial ferry operators plying routes from Ireland. These boats, while not specifically cetacean-watching trips, provide stable viewing platforms through potentially rewarding waters: be it domestic, *i.e.* between Ireland and the British mainland; or further afield, *i.e.* Ireland to France.

ROSSLARE–PEMBROKE,
DUBLIN–HOLYHEAD,
ROSSLARE–CHERBOURG/ROSCOFF
www.irishferries.com

ROSSLARE–FISHGUARD,
DUN LAOGHAIRE/DUBLIN–HOLYHEAD
www.stenaline.co.uk

CORK–ROSCOFF
www.brittany-ferries.co.uk

Locations: Cetaceans

The North Sea coastal region of Britain is relatively rich in terms of cetacean species, with a distinct bias towards species diversity and abundance the further north you go. Eight species are recorded regularly.

Minke Whale – regular in small numbers; mainly June–October.

Harbour Porpoise – widespread, and reasonably common; numbers peaking July–November.

Bottlenose Dolphin – locally fairly common in the north, but uncommon further south; numbers peaking during the summer months.

White-beaked Dolphin – the most common dolphin in the region, occurring mainly offshore, June–September.

White-sided Dolphin – regular but predominantly offshore and only rarely seen from the coast, July–September.

Risso's Dolphin – widely distributed in the north of the region; mainly recorded in July–September off the North Caithness coast and the Pentland Firth.

Long-finned Pilot Whale – fairly common in the north of the region, mainly recorded offshore in June–January.

Killer Whale – recorded annually as far south as the Farnes, mainly in the summer months in inshore locations, appearing to coincide with the Common Seal pupping season; offshore, recorded mostly in winter months.

A number of uncommon species have been recorded in the region, including enigmatic beaked whales, and charismatic species like Humpback and Sperm Whale.

Moray Firth, NE Scotland

The Moray Firth is, alongside Cardigan Bay in Wales, one of the premier sites in Britain to see Bottlenose Dolphins from both the shore and at sea by boat. They may be seen distantly from bays and headlands right around the periphery of the Firth (Findhorn Bay, Burghead, Lossiemouth, Portknockie, Spey Bay etc.). However, sightings are concentrated on where there are ideal feeding conditions for dolphins such as choke-points where narrow channels create rapid tidal currents on a daily basis. At these locations the animals feed close inshore, and may indulge in spectacular acrobatics.
The best of these is the entrance to Inverness Firth between Chanonry Point (NH 748557) and Fort George (NH 762565), where Bottlenose Dolphins are seen daily; other locations include the entrance to Cromarty Firth between North (NH 806690) and South Sutors (NH 807671); and the entrance to Beauly Firth between North (NH 650480) & South Kessock (NH 645467).

Regular boat trips are available to see the dolphins in the Moray Firth. Effort should be concentrated, especially when looking from land-based sites, during the three hours either side of high tide in order to coincide with the optimum feeding conditions for the animals and hence the most activity. Harbour Porpoise and Minke Whale are both regularly seen, especially in the outer reaches of the Moray Firth.

Girdleness, Aberdeenshire

Grid ref: NJ 968055 (unsurfaced car park)
Nearest train station: Aberdeen (2 miles)

Situated at the point at which the River Dee reaches the North Sea at Aberdeen city docks, Girdleness is a regular site for both Harbour Porpoise and Bottlenose Dolphins throughout the year; the dolphins both in and outside the harbour mouth, and the porpoises further out in the open sea. Other species are seen sporadically in the summer months, such as Minke Whale and White-beaked Dolphin, and a good range or rarer species have been recorded including Fin, Humpback and Killer Whales.

Parking is available on Greyhope Road at the remains of the Torry Battery for views over the harbour mouth. Further along Greyhope Road the Girdleness Lighthouse provides a good viewing point looking towards the open sea.

Flamborough Head, East Yorkshire

Grid ref: TA 254706 (car park)
Nearest train stations: Bempton (5 miles)

While not as species-diverse as more northerly waters in the region, Flamborough nevertheless provides a good possibility of seeing Harbour Porpoise, which gather close inshore May–September, and the chance of a Minke Whale in late summer. Other cetacean species have been recorded in the past, and the abundant birdlife just offshore should ensure that looking for cetaceans will not be uneventful. Access is from Lighthouse Road (B1259) – park at the car park at the end of the road, and walk out to view the sea from the cliff-top.

Whale-watching by boat

Operators are concentrated on the Moray and Cromarty Firths.

www.cromarty-ferry.co.uk
www.ecoventures.co.uk
www.geminiexplorer.co.uk
www.inverness-dolphin-trips.co.uk

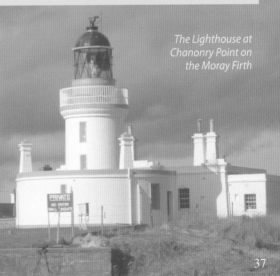

The Lighthouse at Chanonry Point on the Moray Firth

Locations: Cetaceans

The archipelagos of Orkney and Shetland in the far north of Scotland are ideally located for seeing cetaceans, being bordered by the Atlantic Ocean and the North Sea, situated relatively close to the continental shelf-edge, and having rich fishing grounds. Between them, Orkney and Shetland have amassed a total of twenty species recorded since 1980 – a remarkable 69% of the species recorded in British waters. Seven species are either present year-round or recorded annually.

Minke Whale – regular in small numbers along the coast and offshore; mainly June–October.

Harbour Porpoise – widespread, and reasonably common; numbers peaking July–October.

White-beaked Dolphin – fairly common, (June–October), but mainly offshore and only occasionally seen from the coast.

White-sided Dolphin – fairly common, (June–October), but mainly offshore and only sometimes seen from the coast.

Risso's Dolphin – widespread and reasonably common; April–November.

Long-finned Pilot Whale – infrequently seen from land; mainly recorded offshore in September–March.

Killer Whale – recorded annually, year-round offshore, and mainly April–September (peak June–August) inshore.

There have been sightings of the following 13 rare species since 1980: Fin, Sei, Humpback, Sperm and Pygmy Sperm Whales; Sowerby's and Cuvier's Beaked Whales; Northern Bottlenose Whale; Beluga; False Killer Whale; and Bottlenose, Short-beaked Common and Striped Dolphins. Pre 1980, a further three species were recorded: North Atlantic Right Whale, Blue Whale and Narwhal.

Ferry routes

Northlink Ferries operate both the Aberdeen–Kirkwall and Aberdeen–Lerwick ferry routes, which depart from Aberdeen or Lerwick harbours in the early evening. There may, therefore, be some opportunity for looking for cetaceans at either end of the voyage while it is still light. (The boat departs Kirkwall in the late evening.) Northlink also operates the Pentland Firth service (Scrabster–Stromness), which makes several crossings during the course of the day.

www.northlinkferries.co.uk

Whale-watching by boat

ORKNEY
www.orkneyboattrips.co.uk
www.seaorkney.webs.com

SHETLAND
www.seabirds-and-seals.com
www.shetlandwildlife.co.uk

Shetland

Cetacean sightings in Shetland come from all points of the compass. The archipelago's coastline is highly fractured with many sheltered voes (inlets), some of which have fairly deep water close inshore. The combination of Shetland's location, highly tidal sounds between the 100+ islands, and rich fishing grounds means that a cetacean sighting is possible from almost any point on the coastline. There is some bias in records towards the eastern side of Shetland which is, generally speaking, sheltered from the prevailing south-westerly Atlantic weather. This may result in a rather less challenging environment for those cetacean species that regularly occur close inshore, such as Harbour Porpoise. Certainly for land-based sightings of Killer Whales, the bulk of records come from the eastern coast and between the various islands – this undoubtedly paralleling the distribution of the Grey and Common Seals upon which these predators feed. There is no better place in Britain to see this magnificent species than Shetland during the summer.

Orkney

The bulk of cetacean sightings in Orkney come from the west coast; probably a reflection of the better vantage points offered by the higher cliffs rather than any significant difference in sea conditions from a cetacean perspective. Sightings may be made from headlands (*e.g.* Cantick Head), and also in the tidal sounds between the various islands themselves.

Offshore can be productive; in addition to commercial boat trips, there is a regular daily ferry route across the Pentland Firth from Stromness in Orkney to Scrabster on the Scottish mainland that provides a good opportunity to look for cetaceans from the comfort and higher elevation of a passenger ferry.

Mousa Sound from the Broch of Mousa, Shetland

Locations: Cetaceans

The waters around the west Scottish mainland and the offshore islands are excellent for cetaceans; 22 species have been recorded in the region since 1980, including a number of extremely rare species. Eleven species are either present year-round or recorded on an annual basis.

Fin Whale – uncommon, but seen annually in the Minches, the sea of Hebrides, and off south-west Scotland.

Minke Whale – fairly common; most sightings July–October

Sperm Whale – uncommon, mainly in deep off-shelf water.

Long-finned Pilot Whale – fairly common, predominantly in deep off-shelf water; April–September.

Killer Whale – uncommon, mainly inshore amongst the islands; May–September.

Risso's Dolphin – widespread; sightings peak August–September.

White-beaked Dolphin – widespread; sightings peak July–September.

White-sided Dolphin – fairly common; July–August.

Short-beaked Common Dolphin – fairly common; May–July.

Bottlenose Dolphin – resident but rather uncommon; sightings peak April–September.

Harbour Porpoise – common inshore resident, numbers peak July–October.

The following species have also been recorded in the region since 1980: Blue, Sei, Humpback and North Atlantic Right Whales; Pygmy Sperm Whale; Sowerby's and Cuvier's Beaked Whales; Northern Bottlenose Whale; Beluga; and Striped and Fraser's Dolphins.

The Minches and Skye

The waters around Skye are good areas to look for cetaceans. The Minch (or North Minch) is the large area of water north of Skye, enclosed to the west by Lewis and to the east by the Scottish mainland. The Lower (or Little) Minch is the channel northwest of Skye that separates it from North and South Uist, Harris and Lewis.

Both Minches can be viewed from any of the headlands or promontories on the shore, although the size of both bodies of water means that land-based observations only just scratch the surface of the areas' potential. The Minch is some 70 miles long and between 20 and 45 miles wide; and the Lower Minch is 15 miles wide. Land-based vantage points include Tiumpan Head (NB 573377) on Lewis, Rua Reidh lighthouse (NG 740919) 13 miles north of Gairloch on the mainland, and on Skye itself, Neist Point (NG 128471) – the latter being a good place to look for Risso's Dolphins in particular.

As well as these land-based vantage points, there is a well-developed wildlife-watching boat industry in the area. with a number of operators based in various locations. The best views of the local cetaceans are often to be had from these boats.

Mull and the Inner Hebrides

The waters around Mull and the Inner Hebrides (Skye is covered above) are productive areas to look for cetaceans – either from suitable vantage points on land or on a commercial boat trip.

HEADLANDS

Tiumpan Head, Lewis
Grid ref: NB 573377

Tiumpan Head is notable primarily for sightings of Risso's Dolphin – the species is resident here. Looking east across the Minch, a deep natural sea trench close inshore, means that this is also a good location for other cetacean species. Minke Whale, White-beaked Dolphin and Harbour Porpoise are all regular here, and there are occasional sightings of predominantly deeper water species such as Long-finned Pilot Whale and White-sided Dolphin. The optimum time to visit is in the summer – access via the A866 from Stornoway, follow the Broker road northeast onto the Eye Peninsula, following the very minor road to its end at the lighthouse.

Ardnamurchan Point, Highland
Grid ref: NM 416675

Ardnamurchan Point is adjacent to the most westerly point of mainland Britain, and sits at the tip of a peninsula that juts out into the Atlantic, affording excellent views over the open sea and across the water to various islands of the Inner Hebrides. Species recorded regularly here include a good range of dolphin species (Bottlenose, Short-beaked Common and Risso's); Harbour Porpoise; and, through the summer months, Minke Whale.

Access is via the (very) minor road (B8007) from Salen to the Ardnamurchan lighthouse that sits on the western tip of the peninsula. Park here, and view the sea from the shelter of the lighthouse compound.

Tiumpan Head

Whale-watching by boat
Unsurprisingly, there is a good choice of operators in this prime location.

THE MINCHES & SKYE
www.arisaig.co.uk
www.hebridean-whale-cruises.com
www.northwestcruises.co.uk
www.porpoise-gairloch.co.uk
www.seatrek.co.uk
www.whalespotting.co.uk

MULL & THE INNER HEBRIDES
www.mullcharters.com
www.mvchalice.com
www.sealife-adventures.com
www.sealifesurveys.com

Ferry routes
The west of Scotland offers a variety of commercial passenger ferry routes that link the many offshore islands and which can be utilised as cetacean-spotting opportunities. Caledonian MacBrayne (generally abbreviated to 'CalMac') run these inter-island services. Although any of these may produce sightings, some routes over deeper water have the potential to be particularly fruitful:

Ullapool–Stornoway – crosses the Minch.

Uig–Tarbert & Uig–Lochmaddy – both routes cross the Lower Minch.

Oban–Lochboisdale & Oban–Castlebay – both routes cross the Hebridean Sea.

www.calmac.co.uk

The Minches

Britain's Seals

Two species of seal occur year-round on Britain's coastline – Grey and Common (or Harbour) Seals. They are both widely distributed, with Grey Seals, for example, being found at all geographic extremities – from the North Cliffs of Cornwall to the islands of Shetland, and even hauled out on the tidal sandbanks of the English Channel off Kent.

A further five species of pinniped (Ringed, Bearded, Harp and Hooded Seals; and Walrus) occur sporadically in Britain, though there is a distinct northern bias to the records that reflects their circumpolar distribution. Their occurrences are unpredictable, but are keenly anticipated amongst mammal-watchers. As always, paying attention to online wildlife news service providers may pay dividends if you hope to catch up with one of these rarely seen species. And it goes without saying that when watching seals at their haul-outs, you should not automatically assume that they are all the expected species – who knows, it may be that you will be the lucky finder of Britain's next Ringed Seal….

An adult Grey Seal in a characteristic resting posture – body bent like a 'blubber banana'. Seals often adopt this posture while resting on rocks and being exposed by the falling tide, seeming to want to lift as much of their body from the water as physically possible.

Common or Harbour Seal

Phoca vitulina

Adult length:	1·3–1·9 m
Pup length:	65–100 cm at birth
Adult weight:	60–150 kg
Pup weight:	8–12 kg at birth

BEHAVIOUR: When hauled out of the water, Common Seals are gregarious and adults may be found in loose, scattered groups at favoured sites. While individual animals may range up to 30 miles in search of food, they often return to these favoured haul-outs. On land, Common Seals are typically very shy, and will not tolerate a close approach, taking to the water the moment they feel threatened.

As pups are able to take to the water soon after birth, adult females usually choose to pup on land with ready access to deep water. Depending on the available local habitat, this may be a beach or a low-lying rock or terrace.

Common Seals feed on a wide variety of inshore fish, cephalopods and crustaceans.

BIOLOGY: Common Seals have a promiscuous mating system. The pups are born in June and July with a spotted adult coat (their white newborn coat having already been shed and re-absorbed in the mothers womb) and are able to swim with their mother almost immediately after birth. The reason for this is necessity – a lot of pups are born on sandbanks at low tide!

STATUS AND DISTRIBUTION:
Common Seal has a near-circumpolar distribution, with distinct subspecies in both the Pacific and the Atlantic oceans. The UK holds approximately 5% of the world, and 50% of the European, population. The species name is something of a misnomer in the UK as Grey Seals outnumber Common Seals by nearly 3:1. Common Seals are prone to periodic outbreaks

OBSERVATION TIPS:
Found year-round in British waters, Common Seals are extremely faithful to their haul-out sites, and with a respectful distance maintained in order not to disturb the animals, good views can be had at these reliable sites.

of Phocine Distemper Virus (PDV), a disease that can prove fatal for large proportions of the population. In 1988, an estimated 50% of the Common Seal population on the east coast succumbed to PDV. Grey Seals do not seem to be affected, though they could be carriers of the virus. In Britain, Common Seals are the characteristic seal of sandflats and tidal estuaries, and in England their distribution is largely defined by these locations on the south and east coasts. In Scotland, they are also found along rocky shores.

IDENTIFICATION: The pelage of Common Seals is variable, with a base colour that can be either light or dark grey, or brown. Some animals may have a reddish, rusty hue to their coats. The underparts may be somewhat lighter than the upperparts, though the fur can be uniformly coloured. Overlaying this base colour is a conspicuous pattern of spots, rings and blotches, normally uniformly distributed on both the upper and underparts.

SIMILAR SPECIES: The two species most likely to be encountered in British waters are Common Seal and Grey Seal (see *page 52* for how to tell them apart). Other pinniped species are encountered only very rarely in Britain (*pages 53–57*), but are distinctive.

'Rusty' form

Typical form

The sexes are not obviously dimorphic. The head-shape and conformation is identical, and diagnostic, especially in comparison with female Grey Seals. Common Seal has a concave or dished face with a short, neat muzzle and a slight but discernible forehead – this can give the species a rather cat-like appearance.

The 'V'-shaped alignment of the nostrils when viewed head-on is distinctive. The eyes are large and set close together; when viewed in profile the eyes are set forward on the head, being one-third of the way back from the muzzle to the rear of the head (see *page 52*).

Female

Pup

ABOVE: Haul-out of Common Seals – showing a range of pelage colours and density of markings.
BELOW: The spotting on the underside of Common Seals is finer and denser than the blotches usual seen on Grey Seals.

ABOVE: Rocky areas are used as haul-outs, especially in Scotland.
BELOW: Common Seal have a 'gentle', cat-like profile, with a distinctive short, well-defined muzzle.

Grey Seal

Halichoerus grypus

Adult length:	1·8–2·1 m
Pup length:	90–105 cm at birth
Adult weight:	105–310 kg
Pup weight:	11–20 kg at birth

BEHAVIOUR: When hauled out of the water, Grey Seals are gregarious and may be found in groups. In the water, they are typically solitary – a Grey Seal encountered close to the shore will often be seen 'bottling' – hanging vertically in the water with just the head visible above the surface (see *page 50*). They can be quite vocal, often uttering a mournful, moaning cry.

Grey Seals are often tolerant of human activity, and may be seen in harbours in some numbers – particularly around fish processing factories or fishing boats that may provide an easy meal.

Grey Seals feed on a wide variety of fish species found in inshore waters, and may on occasion take seabirds from the surface of the water. They are opportunistic feeders, and have been recorded taking species as large as Great Black-backed Gull.

BIOLOGY: Grey Seals are polygynous, with males competing actively with one another for the chance to mate with several females. This competition usually consists of vocalisations and physical posturing, but may sometimes break into physical contact.

The pups, born between September and December, are restricted to rocky beaches or the foreshore above the high-water mark for the first 3–4 weeks of their lives while they moult their initial yellowish-white, fluffy coat. Females usually choose a remote and inaccessible site on land to pup. However, this is not always the case as pups are occasionally encountered in accessible places. The mother usually remains in close attendance.

OBSERVATION TIPS:
Found year-round in British waters, Grey Seals should be looked for either as a head bobbing above the water, or as an entire animal hauled out from the sea, often in tightly-packed groups. 'Urban' locations, such as fishing harbours (*e.g.* Lerwick in Shetland), may be good places to get close views.

STATUS AND DISTRIBUTION:
Grey Seals are found in the north-west and north-east Atlantic, and in the Baltic. In the UK, they occur along the Atlantic coast from Cornwall to Shetland, and in smaller numbers along the east coast as far south as Kent – but are largely absent from the south coast. The majority are found on Scottish mainland and island coasts.

Globally, Grey Seals are one of the rarest seals in the world, the UK holding approximately 40% of the world, and 95% of the European, population.

IDENTIFICATION: While the pelage of Grey Seals varies widely from reddish-tan to dark greyish-black, most adult Grey Seals are grey on the upperparts and somewhat paler on the underparts, with irregular darker blotches and spots mainly on the upperparts. Adult males may become darker with age. Younger animals are usually paler than adults.

The sexes are dimorphic – adult male Grey Seals are extremely distinctive animals, being bulkier than the females and with a diagnostic head-shape – the top of the muzzle is convex and long, giving a 'Roman-nosed' impression in profile.

Male

Female

Adult females are smaller, slimmer and less bull-necked than males. Although their head-shape is similar to the that of males, the top of the muzzle is usually less convex and normally flat. However, in some individuals it may be concave, giving rise to potential confusion with Common Seal.

Newborn pups are a creamy, yellowish-white, and have a fluffy coat for the first 2–4 weeks of their lives. This becomes increasingly discoloured with the passage of days until it is replaced with a sleek, dense fur similar to the pelage of a pale female.

In both sexes, the nostrils are widely separated when viewed head-on, and are almost parallel – forming two neat vertical lines when closed. The eyes are positioned midway between the tip of the muzzle and the back of the head (see *page 52*).

SIMILAR SPECIES: The two species most likely to be encountered in British waters are Grey Seal and Common Seal (see *page 52* for how to tell them apart). Other pinniped species are encountered extremely rarely in Britain (*pages 53–57*) but are individually distinctive and unlikely to be misidentified.

ABOVE: Grey Seal bottling – seals often hang motionless in the water with their head above the surface.

BELOW: Bull Grey Seals may be aggressive towards one another, with fights often leading to minor bloodshed.

ABOVE: Grey Seals are innately curious, and will often spend some time watching a human on the shore, occasionally even matching the observer's progress along the coast for some distance. In this regard they seem to be particularly fascinated by dogs – an interest matched by many dogs' interest in seals.
BELOW: Haul-out of Grey Seals – showing a range of pelage colours and density of markings.

Differentiating Common and Grey Seals

To separate Common Seal from Grey Seal reliably, attention should be focused on the head of the animal in question.

Grey Seal typically has a convex, or at least flat, long muzzle, giving a doleful, Roman-nosed appearance.

The alignment of the nostrils when viewed head-on is diagnostic – **Grey Seal** nostrils are vertically aligned parallel slits when closed.

Grey Seal – female

Grey Seal – male

Grey Seal – male

Common Seal

Compare also the position of the eyes when the head is seen in profile. **Grey Seal** eyes are halfway between the tip of the muzzle and the back of the head; **Common Seal** eyes are set one third of the way back from the muzzle to the back of the head – much further forward than in Grey Seal.

Common Seal

Common Seal has a much more concave or 'dished' face with a shorter, neater muzzle – they look 'friendlier'.

Common Seal nostrils are diagonal, forming a small, neat V shape. (This feature is easily recalled if one imagines a derogatory two-fingered hand-gesture as being common…)

Other differences are more subjective, but may be helpful for more distant views. Grey Seals (*front*) are larger and bulkier than Common Seals (*behind*), and tend to be more two-toned – distinctly dark on the upperparts and pale on the underparts, and with darker spots mostly on the upperparts. The Common Seal's pelage is more uniformly spotted all over. The 'Grey' part of the Grey Seal's name is unhelpful, as both Grey and Common Seals vary in colouration – and this natural variation is compounded by the differences in colour depending on whether the animal is wet or dry, or whether it is moulting.

RARE SEALS

Walrus *Odobenus rosmarus*

Adult length:	>3·6 m
Adult weight:	>1,200 kg

IDENTIFICATION: Walrus are unmistakable – they are large, stocky and bull-necked pinnipeds with thick, rough and creased skin. In older males the skin on the neck and chest may have warty nodules. The ground colour varies, both with age and the ambient temperature – younger animals are dark with almost black skin; adults are cinnamon brownish-grey, and become paler with age. When hot, the animal's skin may become suffused with blood giving it a reddish, 'sunburnt' appearance.

The nostrils are set on top of the muzzle; there is a profusion of short, stiff pale whiskers; and the eyes are small, appear bloodshot, and are set far apart. The tusks for which the Walrus is well-known are present in both sexes, though longer (up to 1m) in adult males. These tusks may often be partially broken off or entirely absent due to the ravages of time and circumstance.

STATUS AND DISTRIBUTION: Walrus has a nearly circumpolar distribution in the Arctic, and is normally found in shallow water or coastal habitats, usually associated with pack ice – although some individuals are known to summer far away from the ice. The species often hauls out on land or ice to rest and moult.

Confirmed records in Britain post 1900: 1920: Out Skerries, Shetland. **1926:** Uyea, North Roe (and other locations in the islands subsequently), Shetland. **1954:** Collieston, Aberdeenshire. **1981:** Yell, Shetland (and elsewhere down the British mainland east coast subsequently). **1986:** Fetlar (and other locations in the islands subsequently), Shetland. **2002:** Hascosay, Shetland.

Ringed Seal *Phoca hispida*

Adult length:	>1·65 m
Adult weight:	50–110 kg

IDENTIFICATION: Similar to Common Seal, the markings on the coat of adult Ringed Seal are, in textbook individuals, distinctively different, with the spots on the upperparts and flanks each being ringed by a circle of paler grey or dirty white. The ground colour of the upperparts varies between individuals in different shades of grey; the underparts are generally unspotted, and are a silvery light-grey. Younger animals that have not reached full adulthood are virtually unspotted, dark grey above and silver below. The body is extremely stout and plump with a relatively small head, a stubby, short muzzle, and large eyes.

STATUS AND DISTRIBUTION: Ringed Seal has a circumpolar distribution, with a strong affinity for pack and land-fast ice in the Arctic basin, Hudson Bay and Strait, and the Bering and Baltic Seas. It is the most common seal in the Arctic region. Adults are largely sedentary year-round, although it is recorded in Iceland in the winter, and due to its similarity with Common Seal, it may be under-recorded in the north of Scotland.

Confirmed records in Britain post 1900: 1901: Aberdeen. **1940**: Isle of Man. **1968**: Whalsay, Shetland (shot). **1990**: Northumberland. **1994**: Scarborough. **1991** & **1995**: Norfolk. **1999**: Mablethorpe, Lincolnshire. **2001**: Yell, Shetland; **2006**. Bonar Bridge, Kyle of Sutherland, Scotland.

Bearded Seal *Erignathus barbatus*

Adult length:	>2·5 m
Adult weight:	>360 kg

IDENTIFICATION: Bearded Seal is a large seal species – long, stout and heavy-set. The head is relatively small for the body, with a broad muzzle and widely spaced nostrils. The whiskers that give the species its name are the colour of ivory and are numerous, long, densely packed together, and, when dry, extravagantly curled at the tips. The ground colour of the pelage varies widely, from light or dark grey to brown. The area around the eyes and muzzle is often pale, and there is occasionally a dark line running from the top of the head down the muzzle between the eyes.

STATUS AND DISTRIBUTION: Bearded Seal has a circumpolar distribution, usually restricted to areas of shifting sea ice. While not considered particularly migratory (they are associated with sea ice, so may make short-distance localised migrations) some individuals have been recorded living a pelagic existence; a tolerance for the open sea that may explain their relative abundance in Britain compared to other Arctic pinniped species.

Confirmed records in Britain post 1900: **1956:** Mainland, Shetland. **1977:** Yell, Shetland; Burra, Shetland. **1981:** Yell, Shetland. **1986:** Ronas Voe, Shetland. **1987:** Weisdale, Shetland; Burra, Shetland; Orkney (possibly one of the Shetland individuals relocating). **1988:** Orkney; Bressay, Shetland. **1993:** Yell, Shetland. **1998:** Lincolnshire. **1999:** Hartlepool, Teesside (two); Isle of Skye. **2000:** Yell, Shetland. **2005:** Fintoen, Orkney; Easter Quarff, Shetland. **2007:** Chanonry Point, Moray Firth. **2008:** Isle of Mull. **2010:** Yell, Shetland; Finstown, Orkney (still present 2011). **2011:** Unst, Shetland; Beadnell Bay, Northumberland; St. Cyrus and (presumed same individual) Firth of Tay, Fife (also present in 2012).

Harp Seal *Phoca groenlandica*

Adult length:	>1·9 m
Adult weight:	>135 kg

IDENTIFICATION: Unmistakable in typical adult pelage, the ground colour is silvery-white with a black (or in the case of females, a dark) ragged-edged hood on the face, and black 'harps' on either flank. These black patches begin at the shoulders and extend down to the pelvis; seen from above they join at the shoulders to form a rough 'V'-shape. Some individuals have incomplete harp patterns, and spotted backs; very rarely animals occur with no harp whatsoever, or with entirely dark ground colour. Sexually immature animals have a grey pelage scattered with dark blotches. Structurally, Harp Seal gives the impression of being a sleek animal. The head is long and pointed, and the muzzle may be somewhat upturned. There is a slight concavity to the forehead when viewed in profile.

STATUS AND DISTRIBUTION: Harp Seals are widespread throughout the Arctic and far North Atlantic oceans, with a range extending from Hudson Bay eastwards to Cape Chelyuskin in northern Russia. The species is highly migratory, and in the past has been seen in large numbers along the Norwegian coast. The reasons are not clear for these periodic invasions, but food shortages, population increases and climate change have all been mooted as possible causes.

Confirmed records in Britain post 1900: **1901:** Hillswick, Shetland. **1902:** Teignmouth, Devon. **1903:** Firth of Forth. **1968:** Ronas Voe, Shetland. **1987:** two individuals, one at Catfirth and one at Hamnavoe, Shetland; River Humber. **1988:** Medway, Kent; Flamborough Head, Yorkshire. **1994:** Holkham, Norfolk; Eastern Scotland. **1995:** Lindisfarne, Northumberland. **2003:** Portland, Dorset. **2008:** Blyth, Northumberland.

Hooded Seal *Cystophora cristata*

Adult length:	2·0–2·6 m
Adult weight:	145–400 kg

IDENTIFICATION: The species owes its name to the fleshy, wide muzzle that droops down over the mouth of adult males. When inflated, this nasal cavity forms a conspicuous 'hood' on the top of the head, significantly altering the profile of the animal. This effect can be further enhanced by the inflation of a large, pinkish-red membrane from within the left nostril. The ground colour of the body is silvery-grey, substantially blotched with irregular dark markings that give the impression of a marbled appearance. These dark markings coalesce on the head to form a wholly dark face and muzzle.

STATUS AND DISTRIBUTION: Hooded Seals are found in the Atlantic region of the Arctic ocean, and in the far north Atlantic to the east of Greenland. Strongly associated with pack ice, it is a partially migratory species that follows the ice as it ebbs and flows according to the seasons. Outside the breeding season, in the spring, individuals may wander widely, and extralimital animals have been found as far away as Portugal and even in California – in entirely the wrong ocean!

Confirmed records in Britain post 1900: 1903: River Lossie mouth, Elgin. **1980**: Haaf Gruney, Shetland. **1989**: Felixstowe, Suffolk. **1991**: Yell, Shetland. **1993**: Norwick, Shetland. **1996**: River Mersey. **1999**: Orkney. **2000**: Lincolnshire. **2001**: Norfolk; Haven beach, Pembrokeshire. **2004**: St Ives, Cornwall; Dunnet Beach, Caithness. **2005**: River Conon mouth, Ross-shire. **2006**: Saunton Beach, Cornwall. **2010**: Newport-on-Tay, Fife (found dead). **2011**: Chapel St Leonards, Lincolnshire.

Britain's Cetaceans

Regularly occurring cetaceans *pages 60–89*

There are a dozen cetacean species that occur regularly in British waters; these include permanently or seasonally resident species that inhabit shallow inshore waters around the coasts and those that occur seasonally further offshore.

Some species are scarcer than others, particularly those that show some preference for deeper water. Although this may in part reflect the relative lack of observer coverage offshore, some species like Humpback Whale and Striped Dolphin are undoubtedly only found in small numbers in British waters.

Those species that show a preference for inshore waters are more predictable in their habits. Some, like Bottlenose

Dolphins, are resident year-round in some locations and may be looked for with a fair degree of confidence both from land and at sea. Others, like Killer Whale, while present off-shore at all times of year, are found in inshore waters only seasonally, and due to their roving hunting habits are less predictable targets for the cetacean-watcher.

The would-be observer is advised to keep abreast of sightings via the Internet and, if possible, any local wildlife observation grapevines. In some areas, like Shetland, sightings of cetaceans attract considerable interest from naturalists and the general public alike, and word soon gets around when there is something of interest to be seen from the shore.

Surely one of the most iconic and easily recognisable of the cetaceans, it comes as a surprise to many that Killer Whales occur annually in some numbers in British waters and can, with luck, be found with a degree of certainty in some northern coastal locations.

Deepwater cetaceans *pages 90–105*

Three species of whale with a preference for deeper water – Sei, Sperm and Northern Bottlenose Whales – may be found in British waters with some regularity, although sightings are by no means predictable and rely heavily upon happy circumstance. A fourth species, Cuvier's Beaked Whale, is seen much less frequently but is probably present though scarce and under-reported; it strands on British and Irish coasts with some regularity, suggesting it may be more common than confirmed at-sea records would suggest.

Sei, Sperm and Northern Bottlenose Whales are occasionally reported, particularly in Scottish inshore waters, but as might be expected sightings predominantly come from along the continental shelf edge some way offshore. The Northern and Western Isles, due to their relative proximity to the shelf edge, provide the best chance of an encounter with one of these species close to land – but this chance is nevertheless still slim. Boat trips away from inshore waters maximize the possibilities of encountering any one of these species.

Regularly occurring cetaceans

Bottlenose Dolphin 1·9–3·9 m
page 78

White-beaked Dolphin
2·0–3·0 m *page 86*

Risso's Dolphin 2·6–3·8 m
page 82

Atlantic White-sided Dolphin
2·0–2·8 m *page 84*

Harbour Porpoise 1·5 m
page 88

Short-beaked Common Dolphin
1·7–2·5 m *page 74*

Killer Whale
or Orca
(female) 5–6 m
page 68

Long-finned Pilot Whale
(male) 3·5–6·5 m
page 72

0   1   2   3
| | metres

Scale 1:50

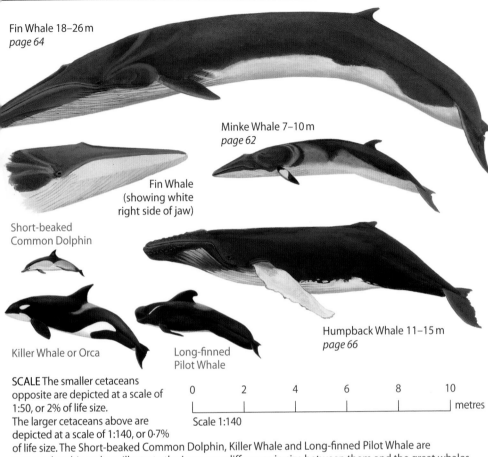

Fin Whale 18–26 m
page 64

Minke Whale 7–10 m
page 62

Fin Whale
(showing white
right side of jaw)

Short-beaked
Common Dolphin

Humpback Whale 11–15 m
page 66

Killer Whale or Orca

Long-finned
Pilot Whale

SCALE The smaller cetaceans opposite are depicted at a scale of 1:50, or 2% of life size.
The larger cetaceans above are depicted at a scale of 1:140, or 0·7%

0		2		4		6		8		10	

metres

Scale 1:140

of life size. The Short-beaked Common Dolphin, Killer Whale and Long-finned Pilot Whale are repeated at this scale to illustrate the immense difference in size between them and the great whales. This is something that is often difficult to appreciate when viewing a great whale, as it only reveals a small proportion of its back at any one time when it surfaces.

The Minke Whale below is shown to illustrate quite how little of a whale is seen at the surface. The portion of the animal below the surface has been faded. Throughout the following accounts all species are depicted in this way to highlight this important point.

Above surface

Below surface

61

Minke Whale

Balaenoptera acutorostrata

Adult length:	7–10 m
Group size:	1–2, occasionally more
Breaching:	Often
Deep dive:	Sinks – tail flukes not raised
Blow:	Light, low, vertical and bushy; often not visible

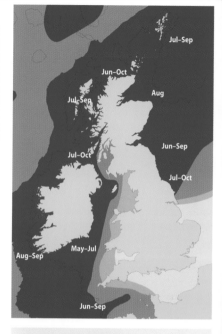

BEHAVIOUR: Most sightings tend to be of single animals, but mother-calf pairs and small aggregations have also been reported – groups of up to 20 animals have been recorded from the Western Isles. Minkes can be elusive when feeding, although can also be inquisitive and will often approach boats. Breaching is often recorded, particularly during rough weather.

Minke Whales hunt a variety of prey including fish (such as herring, cod, mackerel and sand eel), squid and crustaceans, by lunge-feeding or engulfing (see *page 24*), favouring locations where there are strong currents or upwellings.

STATUS AND DISTRIBUTION:

Minke Whales occur worldwide, though seem to have a preference for cooler waters on the continental shelf at depths of 200 m or less. It is therefore little surprise that they are frequently seen during summer and autumn in coastal waters around the whole of Britain, though only rarely in the southern half of the North Sea (south of Yorkshire) and the eastern half of the English Channel. Numbers are greatest off the west coast of Scotland, in particular around the Western Isles. In the Irish Sea, Minke Whales are mainly found on the western side to the south of the Isle of Man. In the North Sea, the Farne Deep and Flamborough Head are regular locations.

OBSERVATION TIPS:

The species has been reported in British and Irish waters in every month of the year, but shows a clear seasonal bias towards the months of May–September. It is during these months that the species may be most frequently seen from land. In late summer, especially in Scotland, they are often seen in association with flocks of Northern Gannets, Manx Shearwaters and Kittiwakes.

Minke Whales are known to come extremely close to the shore on occasion, giving those fortunate enough to be in the right place at the right time superlative views for which binoculars are not necessarily required. A walk in the early evening on a calm summer's day along the shores of the Northern or Western Isles may be amply rewarded.

A Minke Whale's surfacing roll is relatively fast. The inconspicuous blow appears at the same time as the head and snout, which emerge at an angle …

… the top of the head and back, forward of the dorsal fin, are the next to show, sometimes with the blow…

…and then the dorsal fin appears…

IDENTIFICATION: The Minke Whale is the smallest baleen whale to be found around Britain, and the only whale that occurs regularly in shallow water and close to land. The upperparts are dark grey (often appearing black); the flanks have a soft dark-grey pattern that fades to white on the belly and the underside of the flippers. A distinctive feature, though only easily seen at close range, is a diagonal white band on the upper surface of the flipper.

DIVE SEQUENCE: When diving, the tail flukes do not break the surface. A typical dive sequence is 5–8 surface rolls with accompanying blows at approximately one-minute intervals followed by a longer dive of about 5 minutes duration.

A Minke Whale rolls to dive

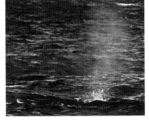

Minke Whale has a slender, streamlined body with a pointed rostrum which is bisected by a single longitudinal ridge beginning in front of the blowholes.

The vertical blow is inconspicuous and is produced at almost the same time as the dorsal fin appears.

The dorsal fin is tall and falcate and located about two-thirds along the back.

SIMILAR SPECIES: The uncommon Fin Whale (*page 64*) and the rare, deepwater Sei Whale (*page 92*) are both larger and have a tall blow. Northern Bottlenose (*page 96*) and Cuvier's Beaked Whales (*page 98*), two other rarely encountered deepwater species, are similar in size and body shape at a distance but both have very different head-shapes from Minke – see *inside back cover*.

...after which the animal rolls quickly... ...exposing the tail-stock which then sinks beneath the surface .

Observing a Minke Whale at sea can be quite hard as it may only roll once or twice before disappearing!

Fin Whale

Balaenoptera physalus

Adult length:	18–26 m
Group size:	1–2, occasionally up to 20
Breaching:	Occasional; huge splash
Deep dive:	Arches tail-stock – tail flukes not raised
Blow:	Dense, tall, column 4–8 m high

BEHAVIOUR: Fin Whales are mostly encountered singly or in pairs and occasionally in small pods or loose aggregations where food is plentiful. They travel at around 18 mph (30 km/h) when cruising, and can reach 30 mph (45 km/h) over short distances. They feed mostly on tiny crustaceans but also on krill, small squid and fish such as herring, mackerel, sand eel and Blue Whiting by filter- or lunge-feeding.

STATUS AND DISTRIBUTION:
Fin Whales occur worldwide, though mainly in temperate and polar seas. The population in British and Irish waters appears to be fluid and dynamic, with locally seasonal peaks of sightings in different locations. While occurring mainly in deeper waters (1,000–4,000 m), sightings on the continental shelf, close to the 500 m contour also occur. In coastal waters, Fin Whales are most commonly sighted between May and August, with a peak in sightings in August, when they may be seen in St George's Channel near the Smalls, in the Sea of Hebrides and the Minches. This peak occurs both on and off the continental shelf, suggesting a genuine increase in numbers rather than just movement within the population.

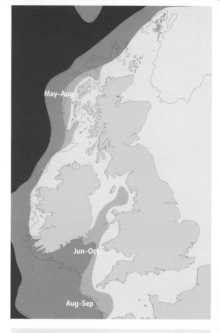

OBSERVATION TIPS:
The best chance of seeing Fin Whales in British waters appears to be at sea in the south-west in August. At this time, the numbers of animals visiting shallow water to feed on shoaling fish peak, coinciding with the most clement conditions for finding and viewing them.

Aggregations of Fin Whales and adults with calves have been reported in the summer months from the south of Ireland and in the western approaches to the English Channel. These sightings, together with many records in December, suggest there may be a resident population in this area – with overwintering animals possibly staying in the area to breed.

The blow appears first…   …then the first part of the back…

IDENTIFICATION: A large (only the Blue Whale is larger) but nonetheless quite slender, streamlined cetacean with a pointed head and a prominent 'swept-back' dorsal fin located three-quarters of the way along the back.

DIVE SEQUENCE: Typically 2–5 blows at approximately 10–20 second intervals followed by a deep dive that averages 10 minutes duration. On very rare occasions the tail flukes may be raised above the surface.

A Fin Whale makes a characteristic shape when commencing a deep dive.

The upperside of the body is dark grey, often with pale chevrons behind the blowholes.

The Fin Whale's unique asymmetrical colouration of the lower jaw can be seen at close range – the left lower jaw is dark; the right white. It is thought that this may be used as a distraction when hunting.

The blow is strong, tall and columnar, taking several seconds to dissipate.

Typical surfacing profile of a Fin Whale.

SIMILAR SPECIES: Confusion with the rare Sei (*page 92* and *inside back cover*) and Blue Whales (*page 109*) is possible. Sei Whales, in comparison, generally have a shorter, more diffuse blow that appears at the same time as the more prominent, sickle-shaped dorsal fin on surfacing. Also, Fin Whales are more likely to arch their tail-stock when diving, whereas Sei Whales haver a tendency to 'sink'. Blue Whales differ in having a small dorsal fin, paler colouration and a mottled body pattern. Unlike Blue Whales, Fin Whales only very rarely raise their tail flukes on diving.

...and then the dorsal fin appears.

A travelling whale then rolls forward and repeats the sequence...

...unless it starts a deep dive, when the shape of the fin and tail-stock are distinctive.

Humpback Whale

Megaptera novaeangliae

Adult length:	11–15 m
Group size:	1–3, sometimes more
Breaching:	Frequent; usually landing on back
Deep dive:	Arches body high prior to raising the tail flukes that have a distinctive, but variable, black and white patterned underside
Blow:	Variable; usually tall – up to 3 m, vertical and 'mushroom'-shaped

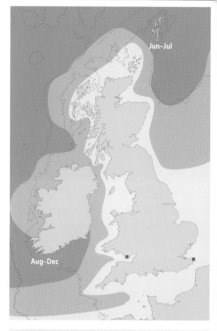

BEHAVIOUR: Humpback Whales are highly vocal and can be very demonstrative, regularly breaching, lob-tailing and slapping their long flippers on the water's surface. They usually travel singly or in very small pods, large congregations usually only being found on the summer feeding grounds. They feed on shoaling fish (such as sand eel, herring, mackerel and anchovy) as well as krill and plankton, sometimes using their flippers to disable fish. Often groups of animals will work together to herd fish, feeding side by side using synchronised lunges or by bubble-netting.

STATUS AND DISTRIBUTION:

Humpback Whales are widely distributed around the world, but are generally considered rare in the eastern North Atlantic after their numbers were severely reduced as a result of over-exploitation by the whaling industry.

Observations from British and Irish waters have increased markedly in the years since the early 1980s, and while the species is still comparatively rarely seen, the increase in sightings hints at a recovering population in the eastern North Atlantic. Sightings are concentrated in 3 main

OBSERVATION TIPS:
Undoubtedly the best chance to see a Humpback Whale is to spend the summer watching from Sumburgh Head, Shetland and the autumn from locations such as Galley Head and Coghna Head in Ireland. The alternative is to take a dedicated trip leaving from SW Ireland.

geographical areas – the Northern Isles south to eastern Scotland; the northern Irish Sea north to south-west Scotland; and the Celtic Sea between southern Ireland, south Wales, and south-west England. Humpback Whales have been seen almost annually in Shetland since 1990 and, although less predictable, the species is regularly seen off south and south-west Ireland.

The blow and head appear first... ... then the first part of the back... ...before the back arches high. A travelling whale then rolls forward and repeats the sequence...

IDENTIFICATION:

Humpbacks are large, stocky whales, black or dark grey in colour with a broad head covered in fleshy tubercules. The pectoral flippers are distinctive, being extremely long and mostly white on both sides. The dorsal fin, situated two-thirds of the way along the back, is usually short and stubby.

DIVE SEQUENCE: When diving, the broad tail flukes raise clear of the water, revealing a 'ragged' irregular trailing edge to the flukes and a black-and-white patterned underside. Dives typically average 6 minutes in duration.

Extremely long, mostly white pectoral flippers.

The body arches steeply prior to a deep dive, exposing the rough-edged tail-stock.

The underside of the tail flukes is variably patterned white, allowing individual animals to be identified.

Dense 'mushroom'-shaped blow

Short, stubby dorsal fin

Typical surfacing profile of a Humpback Whale.

SIMILAR SPECIES: Although similar to several other rorquals in size, such as the rarely seen Sperm Whale *(page 94)* and extremely rare North Atlantic Right Whale *(page 109)*, Humpback Whales are easily separated by their distinctive flippers, fluke pattern and surfacing sequence.

…unless it starts a deep dive, when the back and tail-stock are arched more steeply…

…and the tail flukes break the surface.

The patterned underside of the flukes is distinctive.

67

Killer Whale or Orca

Orcinus orca

Adult length:	5–9 m
Group size:	Family groups of 2–30
Breaching:	Frequent; leaps near-vertically
Deep dive:	Tail flukes not raised
Blow:	Relatively tall and bushy

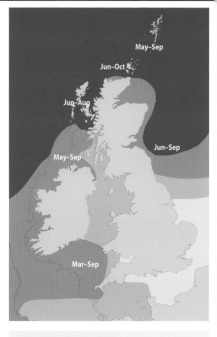

May–Sep
Jun–Oct
Jun–Aug
May–Sep
Jun–Sep
Mar–Sep

BEHAVIOUR: There appear to be two distinct populations of Killer Whale found in British waters, differing in distribution according to their preferred food source. One population appears primarily to inhabit off-shore deep water, where they hunt fish such as herring and mackerel. The other lives closer inshore in shallow water, where their diet is more varied and opportunistic – hunting seals along the coastline, but also taking sea-duck and auks from the surface. They may also attack other whales and dolphins.

STATUS AND DISTRIBUTION:

Killer Whales are found worldwide, although they are most abundant at sub-polar latitudes. Recent studies suggest that there may be more than one species involved.

Recorded all around Britain, although there are very few records from the English Channel or the central and southern North Sea, Killer Whales are most commonly seen in the north and west of Scotland, and in the northern North Sea (*e.g.* the Farne Islands). In recent years, sightings from the Northern Isles (in particular Shetland) have become almost commonplace. Sightings occur year-round, but show a peak from May–September. Photo-identification studies have shown some individuals to be site-faithful for more than ten years. During November–March,

OBSERVATION TIPS:

The most reliable area of the British Isles in which to see Killer Whales is Shetland in June and July. At this time sightings of the species peak, coinciding with the pupping of Common Seals (*page 44*). Tight flocks of gulls circling and feeding on small areas of water just offshore may be a clue that there are hunting Killer Whales in the near vicinity – the detritus left after a kill often proves irresistible to local scavengers.

Killer Whales are regularly seen at sea associating with mackerel purse-seine fishing boats. Animals often appear just after the boats start to haul in their nets to feed opportunistically upon fish spilling from them, suggesting they associate the sound with an easy meal.

The blow, head and dorsal fin appear at the same time…

… then the first part of the back…

…followed by the prominent dorsal fin…

IDENTIFICATION:

Despite its name, the Killer Whale is actually the world's largest dolphin, and perhaps the most striking and familiar cetacean of all. The stocky, sleek black body, white eye-patch and prominent dorsal fin are unmistakable. Most animals show a clear grey 'saddle' patch behind the dorsal fin.

When a Killer Whale rolls the grey 'saddle' behind the dorsal fin is distinctive, though variable between individuals.

The bushy blow is not always easy to see.

Females and immature animals are significantly shorter in body length than males, with smaller, sickle-shaped dorsal fins.

Typical Killer Whale surfacing profile.

Fin shape and size varies depending upon the age and gender of the individual. Adult males are the most distinctive, with broad, triangular dorsal fins reaching up to 2 m in height.

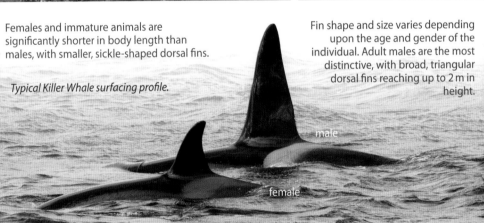

male

female

SIMILAR SPECIES: Confusion is unlikely with any other species, with the possible exception of a Risso's Dolphin (*page 82*) seen distantly, or the extremely rare False Killer Whale (*page 114*).

Female/immature

Male

...after which the tail-stock is arched before diving.

The shape of the dorsal fin depends upon age and gender – adult males are unmistakable.

69

ABOVE: Killer Whales spend most of their lives in discrete family groups, so most sightings will involve multiple individuals. Photo-identification studies in Shetland have established that the same groups return to the islands year after year.

BELOW: Killer Whales may come close to the shore when hunting seals, allowing superlative views.

ABOVE: These powerful predators are capable of swimming at speeds in excess of 30 mph (45 km/h).
BELOW: Killer Whales regularly breach, lob-tail and spy-hop.

Long-finned Pilot Whale

Globicephala melas

Adult length:	3·5–6·5 m
Group size:	Family groups of 2–50
Breaching:	Regular; at various angles
Deep dive:	Tail flukes not raised
Blow:	Low and distinctly bushy; often not visible

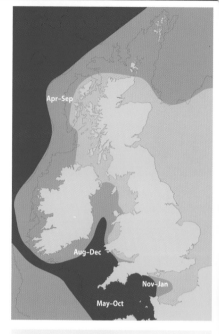

Apr–Sep

Aug–Dec

Nov–Jan

May–Oct

BEHAVIOUR: Long-finned Pilot Whales are usually seen in family groups. They feed mostly at night, spending much of the day travelling slowly (at around 2 mph (3 km/h), or logging at the surface. Despite their languid nature they are inquisitive and demonstrative animals, often appearing close to ships, when they may spy-hop, tail-slap (see *page 25*) or flipper-slap. They also breach regularly and often associate with Bottlenose Dolphins. Long-finned Pilot Whales feed predominantly on cuttlefish and other small squid, but also shoaling fish such as Blue Whiting. Their distribution at any one time is linked to the abundance of their prey. Long-finned Pilot Whales are prone to mass stranding. Why they do so is not fully understood, but may be due to their tight social structure, with all the animals in a group following a lead individual that has become disorientated for some reason.

STATUS AND DISTRIBUTION:

Long-finned Pilot Whales are found in the temperate and sub-polar seas of both hemispheres. Commonly found in deep North Atlantic waters, with a distinct preference for the continental shelf slope along the 1,000 m depth contour, the species is also seen with some regularity in shallower inshore waters, occasionally even entering relatively enclosed bays.

OBSERVATION TIPS:
Present all year, most commonly seen in the deeper water over the edge of the continental shelf, but also fairly common in the offshore waters of SW Britain and the English Channel. A watch from any headland in these areas on a calm late summer or autumn day may be rewarded.

Most common around northern and western Scotland and the south-west of England, Long-finned Pilot Whales have been recorded year-round, though sightings peak in July–August. They are also fairly common offshore in the southern Irish Sea. There seems to be an easterly movement in the English Channel during the autumn, with animals remaining until the early spring.

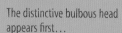

The distinctive bulbous head appears first...

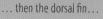

... then the dorsal fin...

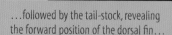

...followed by the tail-stock, revealing the forward position of the dorsal fin...

IDENTIFICATION:
The Long-finned Pilot Whale is easily identified by its distinctive shape and behaviour. They are glossy black in colour, with a narrow white underbelly.

DIVE SEQUENCE: On surfacing, the bulbous, rounded head and distinct bushy blow precedes a robust body with the dorsal fin set well forward on the back.

Fin positions of Bottlenose Dolphin (TOP) and Long-finned Pilot Whale (BOTTOM).

Pilot whales often spy-hop.

The dorsal fin is distinctly broad-based, a feature that is most striking in muscular mature males. Immature animals have pointed, dolphin-like dorsal fins that, being located relatively close to the head, should distinguish them from most other dolphin species.

male

female

SIMILAR SPECIES: The forward position of the dorsal fin is diagnostic of this species in the region. A poorly seen Bottlenose Dolphin (*page 78*), which often associates with pilot whales, Risso's Dolphin (*page 82*) or the extremely rare False Killer Whale (*page 114*) can all appear similar to a female/immature pilot whale. However, these species have a centrally located dorsal fin and head-shapes that are unlike a pilot whale. Any sighting of a bulbous head and forward-positioned dorsal fin will confirm the presence of a Long-finned Pilot Whale.

Male   Female/immature

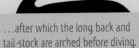

...after which the long back and tail-stock are arched before diving.

The shape of the dorsal fin depends upon age and gender. Males have a distinctive broad 'smurf hat' fin; females/immatures are more dolphin-like.

73

Short-beaked Common Dolphin

Delphinus delphis

Adult length:	1·7–2·5 m
Group size:	1–500, occasionally more
Behaviour:	Very active; fast; acrobatic

BEHAVIOUR: Short-beaked Common Dolphins are fast, energetic animals. When travelling they frequently porpoise clear of the water and can reach speeds in excess of 35 mph (60 km/h). They will actively seek out the bow-wave or wake of moving vessels. They are highly social animals and feed mainly on shoaling fish such as mackerel, sprat, pilchard and Blue Whiting. The average pod size around Britain is about 20, although in the Bay of Biscay groups of more than 500 have been seen. In deeper waters, Short-beaked Common Dolphins sometimes associate with other species – principally with Striped Dolphins, but occasionally with Bottlenose Dolphins and Long-finned Pilot Whales.

STATUS AND DISTRIBUTION:

Short-beaked Common Dolphins are found in the world's warm temperate and tropical seas. They are the most abundant cetacean in British waters, occurring mainly on the deeper side of the 200 m contour to the south and west. The species is common in the western half of the English Channel, the southern Irish Sea, the Sea of Hebrides, and the southern part of the Minch. In some years it occurs farther north and east in shelf seas, extending its range to the northern Western Isles, the Northern Isles, and into the northern North Sea. The species is rare in the eastern half of the English Channel, and only occasionally seen in the central and southern North Sea.

OBSERVATION TIPS:
Short-beaked Common Dolphins tend to show a preference for deeper waters, but may be found close inshore. The first indication of their presence is often the splashes created by the exuberant activity of a group of animals. Watching in late summer from the headlands of W Scotland, SW England, Wales or Ireland may bring reward. Summer ferry crossings and dedicated trips into the St George's Channel, the Irish Sea or around the Western Isles offer a much better chance of an encounter.

Present in British waters year-round, there appears to be a seasonal movement into our waters in the months May–October, with a corresponding peak in sightings at this time.

Larger groups of Short-beaked Common Dolphins are typically made up of a number of smaller family pods travelling together.

IDENTIFICATION:

A streamlined dolphin with a long, slender, dark beak and a tall, falcate dorsal fin. The key identification feature is a characteristic 'figure-of-eight' pattern on the flanks.

An active group of Short-beaked Common Dolphins.

At close range, the front half can be seen to be tawny-yellow or brown, and the rear half pale grey. Close views may also reveal the thin black stripe that runs from the beak to the flipper, and a second dark stripe that runs from the beak to the eye.

The dorsal fin often has a pale patch in the centre.

The tawny-yellow flank pattern can often be seen on an individual that is only just breaking the surface.

SIMILAR SPECIES: Short-beaked Common Dolphins seen distantly, or in poor weather conditions, may be mistaken for the slimmer, deepwater Striped Dolphin (*page 104*) or possibly the more robust Atlantic White-sided Dolphin (*page 84*). However, any view of the distinctive flank pattern will immediately distinguish Short-beaked Common Dolphin from all other species.

Lots of low leaps and a considerable amount of splashing are characteristic. At a distance the 'clumped' nature of the group and consistently low height of the splashes are good indicators of this species.

ABOVE: Porpoising Short-beaked Common Dolphins – the tawny-yellow and grey figure-of-eight pattern on the flanks is distinctive on these acrobatic animals.
BELOW: Bow-riding Short-beaked Common Dolphins – their propensity for this behaviour allows for close and often prolonged views.

ABOVE: The tawny-yellow flank pattern is even apparent on an animal coming towards you.
BELOW: Short-beaked Common Dolphins are gregarious, highly social creatures, and young may be seen associating closely with their mother.

Bottlenose Dolphin

Tursiops truncatus

Adult length:	1·9–3·9 m
Group size:	1–50
Behaviour:	Highly active, capable of great speed and amazing acrobatics

BEHAVIOUR: Bottlenose Dolphins are very active, curious animals that can travel at great speed. They are capable of amazing acrobatics, and frequently breach, lob-tail and body-surf, as well as ride the bow-wave or wake of boats. The Bottlenose Dolphin is a highly social species, most commonly seen around Britain in groups of between five and 25 individuals which, on occasion, join to form larger groups. They have a very varied diet of fish, squid and shellfish. Bottlenose Dolphins are quite aggressive towards one another and also towards other cetaceans, especially Harbour Porpoises, which they will attack and kill – not for food, but because they are regarded as competitors for food resources.

STATUS AND DISTRIBUTION:

Bottlenose Dolphins have a worldwide distribution in temperate and tropical seas, reaching the northern limit of their range around Iceland. The species occurs both inshore and out to sea in deeper water. It is locally common inshore around much of Britain and Ireland, often favouring river estuaries, headlands and sandbanks where there are strong tidal currents.

Well-known 'hot-spots' for Bottlenose Dolphins are in north-east Scotland (particularly the Moray Firth south to the Firth of Forth), south-west Scotland, the Irish Sea (particularly Cardigan Bay), and in the English Channel (particularly off the Dorset coast). Although present at most known inshore sites year-round, numbers are

OBSERVATION TIPS:
This is one of the most 'reliable' cetacean species in the UK as it is both relatively sedentary at some inshore locations and innately curious about human activity. There are a number of shore-based sites where the species is reguarly seen and quite few boat operators who run trips to see Bottlenose Dolphins (see *pages 26–41*).

greatest around Britain during May-September. There is regional variation in this frequency; for example, in the English Channel there appears to be an annual east-west seasonal migration, with animals moving east from Cornwall to as far as East Sussex in the spring, and returning back to the south-west of England in the late autumn.

For a large animal Bottlenose Dolphins can be surprisingly unobtrusive when not highly active, the only indication of their presence sometimes being just a large dorsal fin breaking surface.

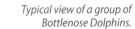

IDENTIFICATION:

The Bottlenose is a large, robust dolphin which, due to its widespread use in aquaria and its popularity with the media, is one of the most familiar of all the cetaceans. The body colouration is uniformly grey above, fading to paler grey flanks and a lighter belly.

Typical view of a group of Bottlenose Dolphins.

The curved forehead leads to a distinctly short and stubby beak – the 'bottlenose'.

The dorsal fin is centrally located, tall, and falcate.

SIMILAR SPECIES: The large size, plain grey colouration, and lack of distinct flank markings distinguish the Bottlenose Dolphin from the other dolphins of the region, such as Short-beaked Common Dolphin (*page 74*) or White-beaked Dolphin (*page 86*). There is a possibility of confusion with Harbour Porpoise (*page 88*) although the size, head-shape, large dorsal fin and different behaviour should distinguish Bottlenose Dolphin from that species.

Bottlenose Dolphins are very noticeable when travelling, with vigorous porpoising and lots of splashes indicating their presence and location. Seen at a distance, groups tend to appear more compact than those of Short-beaked Common Dolphin.

ABOVE: There is a strong bond and a long-lasting association between a mother Bottlenose Dolphin and her calf.
BELOW: Bottlenose Dolphins will investigate small boats and will regularly bow-ride a travelling vessel.

ABOVE: Groups of dolphins will often 'play' especially after feeding, when they will leap, somersault and tail-slap.

BELOW: Although Bottlenose Dolphins usually feed alone they will often work together, herding fish by trapping them against the surface or by driving them to the shoreline.

Risso's Dolphin

Grampus griseus

Adult length:	2·6–3·8 m
Group size:	1–15
Behaviour:	Can be energetic, but usually seen logging or travelling slowly.

BEHAVIOUR: Risso's Dolphins are gregarious animals, spending much of the day logging or travelling leisurely, sometimes in a chorus line, prior to spending the night feeding, mainly on octopus and squid. They are inquisitive and demonstrative cetaceans; often breaching, spy-hopping, and tail-slapping – although most observations in British waters involve slow-travelling or logging animals. They can be aggressive, often using their flippers, fins or flukes (and sometimes their entire body) to strike one another. Pods comprise generally less than 15 individuals, though larger nursery pods with calves swimming alongside their mothers may occasionally be encountered. Risso's Dolphins sometimes associate with Long-finned Pilot Whales.

STATUS AND DISTRIBUTION:

Risso's Dolphin is primarily a warm water species, found in tropical and temperate waters worldwide, with a preference for shelf waters 200–1,000 m in depth. In British waters the species has a distinctly westerly bias, being found down the entire western Atlantic seaboard from Shetland in the north to the Southwest Approaches in the south-west.

The main population in the region is found around the Western Isles, although the species is also seen with some regularity in the Northern Isles and the Irish Sea.

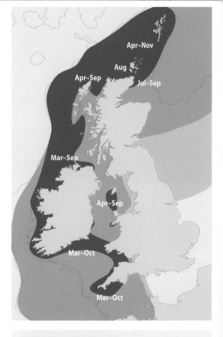

OBSERVATION TIPS:
Although found year-round in British waters, numbers peak May–October. During May–July, the numbers tend to be greatest offshore in deeper water, but in August–September the species is regularly recorded closer inshore, either singly or in small aggregations – sometimes involving mother/calf pairs. Away from the Western and Northern Isles, the headlands of SW Britain and Ireland and those of the Lleyn Peninsula and Pembrokeshire in Wales offer good prospects of a sighting. Risso's Dolphins are sometimes seen from boat trips that venture offshore near to the Celtic Deep.

The species is rare in the North Sea and the English Channel, except for in the westernmost part.

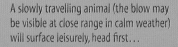

A slowly travelling animal (the blow may be visible at close range in calm weather) will surface leisurely, head first…

… followed by the back and dorsal fin…

IDENTIFICATION:

Risso's Dolphin is unlikely to be mistaken at close range on account of its distinctive shape and colouration – being a large, robust dolphin with a blunt, rounded head that has a slight melon and lacks a beak.

The body is uniformly dark grey to white in colouration, depending on maturity; adults become paler and more heavily scarred as they get older, although the dorsal fin and adjacent back usually remain distinctly darker. The often extensive scarring is the result of conflict with other Risso's Dolphins.

A young Risso's Dolphin is dark grey and unscarred.

The centrally located dorsal fin is tall and falcate.

SIMILAR SPECIES: From a distance or in poor viewing conditions, Risso's Dolphin could be confused with Bottlenose Dolphin (*page 78*) or female Long-finned Pilot Whale (*page 72*) (with which they sometimes associate). However, a combination of the Risso's Dolphin's bluntly rounded forehead, lack of distinct beak and much larger, more 'hooked' and centrally located dorsal fin should rule out both of those species.

…after which the animal assumes its characteristic profile of head, back and swept-back dorsal fin…

…before rolling over slowly exposing the fin and tail-stock (occasionally fluking).

Atlantic White-sided Dolphin

Lagenorhynchus acutus

Adult length:	2·0–2·8 m
Group size:	1–50
Behaviour:	Powerful, energetic and acrobatic; regularly breaches and lob-tails; avoids boats

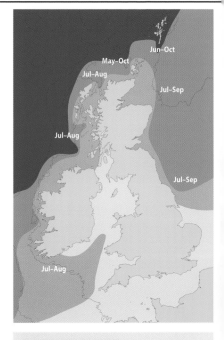

BEHAVIOUR: Atlantic White-sided Dolphins are fast and powerful. They are often encountered as groups of 2–15 animals travelling at speeds in excess of 9 mph (14 km/h), showing only their upper backs and tall, sickle-shaped dorsal fin as they scythe through the water. When not travelling they can be energetic and highly acrobatic, often lob-tailing, and with exuberant displays of breaching and tail-slapping. Larger aggregations of several hundred individuals, formed from smaller groups, are not uncommon (particularly in deeper offshore waters) where they gather to feed on a variety of fish that includes whiting, mackerel and Lanternfish.

STATUS AND DISTRIBUTION:

The Atlantic White-sided Dolphin is only found in the temperate and sub-polar seas of the North Atlantic, with a greater abundance in the north of its range. They favour cooler waters, 100–500 m deep, along the continental shelf edge, with a preference for locations with marked relief, such as deep canyons. In Britain, the main distribution is concentrated around the Northern Isles (where they may come close to shore) and the southern end of the Sea of Hebrides and the north and central North Sea. The species is resident in the deep waters north of Scotland, particulary in the Faeroe–Shetland Channel, and appears to enter the North Sea mainly in summer.

OBSERVATION TIPS:
Whilst reported in British and Irish waters year-round, there is a distinct peak in sightings in shallow inshore waters during June–September, peaking in August. Some time spent in August looking from Sumburgh Head towards Fair Isle provides the best opportunity of a lucky sighting from land. Ferries to the Western or Northern Isles, or a boat trip to the west of Orkney may offer a better chance.

Atlantic White-sided Dolphins are also occasionally seen in the southern Irish Sea and to the west of the English Channel, but rarely in the the northern Irish Sea; the southern North Sea and the English Channel.

When travelling all that is usually seen is the upper back and dorsal fin.

IDENTIFICATION:

A large, robust dolphin with a markedly thick tail-stock. It has a tall, sickle-shaped dorsal fin located halfway along the back. The short beak, back and dorsal fin are all dark-slate coloured, the flanks pale grey, and the belly white.

Two Atlantic White-sided Dolphins in typical travelling profile.

The principal identification feature is the sharply defined white patch on the flanks, which extends along the tail-stock as an elongated yellow or tan stripe.

SIMILAR SPECIES: At long range the Atlantic White-sided Dolphin could be mistaken for several other species, although the well-defined yellow or tan flank stripe is diagnostic. The most likely confusion is with the White-beaked Dolphin (*page 86*) that is a similar size and has a similar dorsal fin. However the White-beaked Dolphin lacks any well-defined flank stripes, and instead has diffuse white or pale markings on the flanks and on the back behind the dorsal fin.

When not travelling Atlantic White-sided Dolphins will regularly tail-slap, breach, and lob-tail.

85

White-beaked Dolphin

Lagenorhynchus albirostris

Adult length:	2–3 m
Group size:	1–20
Behaviour:	Powerful and active; regularly breaches and lob-tails; not shy; follows boats

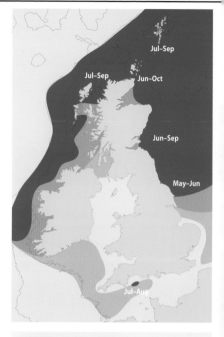

BEHAVIOUR: White-beaked Dolphins are powerful, fast and very active, regularly breaching and tail-slapping. They regularly travel at speeds of up 7 mph (12 km/h), even reaching in excess of 18 mph (30 km/h) over short distances. They seek out small boats and larger ships to bow-ride, with a preference for vessels that are travelling at speed! White-beaked Dolphins tend to occur in small pods, with up to 20 individuals being recorded together. They often hunt co-operatively, feeding mainly on a wide variety of fish that includes mackerel, herring, sand eel and flatfish, though squid and octopus are also taken.

STATUS AND DISTRIBUTION:

White-beaked Dolphins are restricted to temperate and sub-polar seas of the North Atlantic in water less than 200 m deep and predominantly in water depths of 50–100 m. The species is common in British waters, with some regional variance in abundance. It is most common in the central and northern North Sea and around the Western Isles, in particular the north Minch and the western Sea of Hebrides. It also occurs occasionally in the St George's Channel and the English Channel and there appears to be a small resident population in Lyme Bay, Dorset, based on year-round sightings.

OBSERVATION TIPS:
White-beaked Dolphins are recorded year-round, but there is a marked increase in sightings from June–September, with a peak in August. The exceptions to this are in the southern North Sea (off eastern England), where the seasonal peak is earlier (May–June). Sumburgh Head, Shetland is perhaps the most reliable location from which to see this species, with numbers at their highest between July and September. Watching from Tiumpan Head, Isle of Lewis and the coast around Aberdeen may prove successful. There are also regular sightings from the Farne Deeps and from the Northumberland coast, though almost certainly the best chance of an encounter is to take a dedicated trip out into Lyme Bay and hope for weather conditions that are conducive for observing cetaceans.

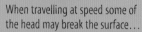

When travelling at speed some of the head may break the surface…

…followed by a typical dolphin roll exposing the back and then the tail-stock.

IDENTIFICATION:

A large, very robust dolphin with a short, thick rounded beak and thick tail-stock. The belly is white as far back as the tail-stock, the dorsal fin is tall and sickle-shaped, and the beak is usually pale grey or white.

The white or pale-grey markings on the flanks are relatively distinctive. In particular, the pale-grey area on the back behind the dorsal fin, gives the impression of a pale 'saddle' and is relatively easy to see on a travelling animal.

SIMILAR SPECIES: At long range the White-beaked Dolphin could be mistaken for several other species, although the diffuse flank patterning and 'saddle' are distinctive. The most likely confusion is with the Atlantic White-sided Dolphin (*page 84*), which is a similar size and has a similar dorsal fin. However, that species can be distinguished by the all-dark upperparts and long, discrete, oval-shaped white patch on the flanks that extends along the tail-stock as a thick yellow/tan stripe.

White-beaked Dolphins regularly tail-slap and breach.

Harbour Porpoise

Phocoena phocoena

Adult length:	1·5–1·7 m
Group size:	1–6
Behaviour:	Lethargic; shy and inconspicuous; usually moves away from boats

BEHAVIOUR: Harbour Porpoises are lethargic, unobtrusive cetaceans, usually sighted alone or in small groups, although larger aggregations are regularly seen in some locations. Their small size, slow movement and shy nature means that, other than in calm conditions, they are easy to overlook. Harbour Porpoises almost never approach boats, usually actively moving away from vessels. Frequently all that is seen is the small dorsal fin breaking the surface but on the rare occasions they do move at any speed they often produce a characteristic 'rooster-tail' of water spray which gives away their location. Harbour Porpoises usually forage independently, though there have been observations of groups feeding collaboratively, herding fish to the surface. They eat small shoaling fish, such as whiting, sprat, herring and sand eel, and regularly take advantage of tidal currents to feed.

STATUS AND DISTRIBUTION:

Harbour Porpoises are found almost exclusively in shallow water over the continental shelf, with a marked preference for coastal inshore waters. While the species has declined across Europe in the past 30 years (including in British waters) it nevertheless remains relatively abundant in Britain, particularly around north-west and north-east Scotland, off south-west England, and around most of Wales.

OBSERVATION TIPS:
Harbour Porpoise occurs in all months of the year, but in many locations there is a seasonal peak in July–September. Other regional variations exist – in the south-west of England sightings peak in December–March, and in the south-east of England in April. It is possible to encounter a Harbour Porpoise at any time around the coast of Britain. Aggregations are regularly seen around the Western and Northern Isles and along the west coast of Scotland. Other good locations include the coastal headlands of Wales (summer), NE Northern Ireland (late summer) and North Devon (winter).

Harbour Porpoises can be seen regularly from St David's Head and in Ramsey Sound, Pembrokeshire (see *page 33*) where they exploit tidal conditions.

The top of the head and back as far back as the dorsal fin appear first in a very shallow roll…

…the head then submerges…

…and the animal submerges, the fin being the last part to remain above the surface.

IDENTIFICATION:

The Harbour Porpoise is the smallest cetacean found in British waters. Though small, it has a robust body with a small, rounded head that lacks a beak. The upperparts are dark grey, fading to lighter grey on the flanks; the underside of the body is white. Calves and juveniles often have brownish backs.

Fin shapes of Bottlenose Dolphin (LEFT) and Harbour Porpoise (RIGHT).

The small, low and triangular dorsal fin is located centrally on the back and, though unobtrusive, it is a good identification feature.

SIMILAR SPECIES: At distance, Harbour Porpoise may be confused with Bottlenose Dolphin (*page 78*), which also shows a centrally located dorsal fin and uniform grey upperparts. However, when seen well, the diminutive size, distinctive shape of the dorsal fin, and its unobtrusive behaviour should distinguish the Harbour Porpoise from all other cetaceans in British waters.

A surfacing Harbour Porpoise can be challenging to spot and observe, being highly unobtrusive in all but the calmest conditions.

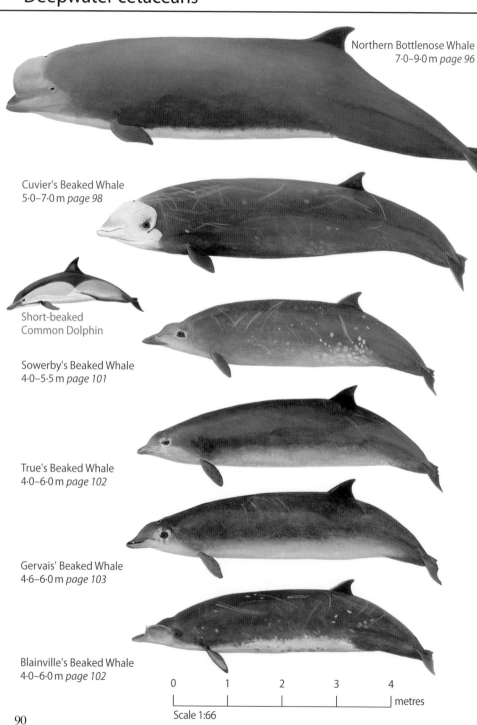

Northern Bottlenose Whale
7·0–9·0 m *page 96*

Cuvier's Beaked Whale
5·0–7·0 m *page 98*

Short-beaked
Common Dolphin

Sowerby's Beaked Whale
4·0–5·5 m *page 101*

True's Beaked Whale
4·0–6·0 m *page 102*

Gervais' Beaked Whale
4·6–6·0 m *page 103*

Blainville's Beaked Whale
4·0–6·0 m *page 102*

0 1 2 3 4
| metres
Scale 1:66

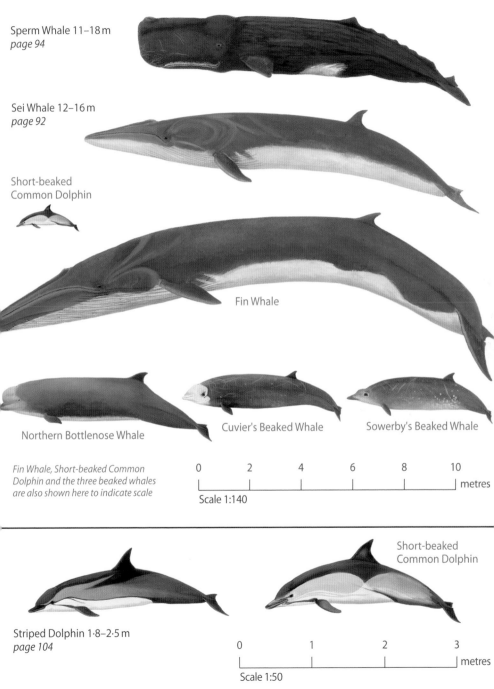

Sperm Whale 11–18 m
page 94

Sei Whale 12–16 m
page 92

Short-beaked
Common Dolphin

Fin Whale

Northern Bottlenose Whale

Cuvier's Beaked Whale

Sowerby's Beaked Whale

*Fin Whale, Short-beaked Common
Dolphin and the three beaked whales
are also shown here to indicate scale*

0   2   4   6   8   10
metres

Scale 1:140

Short-beaked
Common Dolphin

Striped Dolphin 1·8–2·5 m
page 104

0   1   2   3
metres

Scale 1:50

Sei Whale

Balaenoptera borealis

Endangered

Adult length:	12–16 m
Group size:	1–2, occasionally more
Breaching:	Seldom; low angle
Deep dive:	Tail flukes not raised
Blow:	Tall thin and vertical, not as robust as Fin Whale

BEHAVIOUR: Sei Whales tend to travel either alone or in pairs. They are fast swimmers, often skim-feeding on plankton just below the surface in a manner that is rather different from other rorquals. When feeding they are quite unobtrusive, with only an occasional blow and top of the dorsal fin being visible. Sei Whales are not as active as either Fin or Minke Whales, breaching only occasionally – when they tend to emerge from the water at a shallow angle and land on their belly. During their typically short dives they rarely descend more than a few metres, and may be tracked by their fluke prints.

STATUS AND DISTRIBUTION:
Sei Whales have a cosmopolitan distribution, but show a preference for temperate and sub-polar waters in both hemispheres. In the eastern North Atlantic, the species appears to be rare, occurring mainly in deep waters from Iceland and Norway south to the Bay of Biscay and the Iberian Peninsula. It is known to be migratory, wintering in the south and spending the summer months off Shetland, the Faeroes, Norway, Bear Island

May–Aug

Jun

OBSERVATION TIPS:
Sei Whale sightings in British waters are sporadic and in the main unpredictable. Their preference for deep water makes land-based sightings less likely – but not impossible, as animals are occasionally seen from island locations such as Shetland.

and Svalbard. Numbers are known to fluctuate from year to year.

In British shelf waters, sightings also fluctuate annually, and are generally rare. The species is mainly reported during July–October. Sightings in British waters are predominantly in deeper water, for example from the Faeroe–Shetland channel in August.

When a Sei Whale surfaces, the blow and fin usually appear at (or almost at) the same time (compare with Fin Whale page 64) …

… then the animal rolls slowly at a shallow angle with the dorsal fin prominent …

IDENTIFICATION:
Sei Whale is a large, dark whale with an upright, sickle-shaped dorsal fin located two-thirds of the way along the back.

Sei Whale is similar in form and colour to a small Fin Whale, but the dorsal fin appears to be proportionally larger than that of Fin Whale.

The blow is quite tall (around 3 m) but neither as tall nor as dense as in Blue or Fin Whales.

A median ridge on the slender head extends from the blowholes almost to the tip of the rostrum.

When feeding or travelling the back and dorsal fin are usually visible for a longer period compared with other rorquals…

…and often 'sink' rather than roll, with the dorsal fin the last part of the animal to remain above the surface. The tail flukes remain below the surface at all times.

DIVE SEQUENCE: When surfacing, the blowholes and dorsal fin appear almost simultaneously.

SIMILAR SPECIES: Sei Whale is easily confused with both Minke (*page 62*) and Fin (*page 64*) Whales and a combination of features is needed to distinguish these species – see *inside back cover*. Compared with Sei Whale, Fin Whale usually has a higher blow which usually appears well before the smaller, more 'swept-back' dorsal fin. Unlike Fin Whales, Sei Whales do not usually arch their tail-stock prior to a deep dive. At close range, the asymmetrical head pattern of Fin Whale is diagnostic. Minke Whales are distinguished from Sei Whales by their smaller size and lack of a prominent blow.

… before gradually sinking …   … with the dorsal fin being the last part visible.

93

Sperm Whale

Physeter macrocephalus

Adult length:	11–18 m
Group size:	1–20, occasionally more
Breaching:	Often; vertical
Deep dive:	Often arches body; tail flukes usually raised
Blow:	Angled forwards to the left

Dec–Feb

BEHAVIOUR: Sperm Whales are gregarious and usually encountered either as widely spread pods of mixed females and immature males, or bachelor males, in groups of often up to 20 or more. They can be quite demonstrative and breach regularly, especially younger animals. Sperm Whales are renowned for diving to tremendous depths to capture deep-water fish, sharks and squid.

STATUS AND DISTRIBUTION:

Sperm Whales have a worldwide distribution in tropical, temperate and sub-polar seas in both hemispheres. A denizen of particularly deep waters, it is considered to be the commonest large whale in this particular habitat. Although numbers were depleted by the whaling industry, the Sperm Whale was not hit as hard as other species. Reports from British waters increased significantly in the 1990s compared with the preceding two decades, suggesting a resurgent population.

Mixed female/immature male pods usually remain in tropical or subtropical waters year-round, but adult and adolescent males travel to higher latitudes, sometimes to the Arctic ice-edge, to feed before returning to the females for the breeding season. It is mainly

OBSERVATION TIPS:
Sightings of Sperm Whale off the continental shelf peak in the summer months, whereas those on the shelf or in coastal waters peak in winter. This reflects acoustic survey data that indicate that it may overwinter in significant numbers off northern Britain during December–February. Offshore surveys suggest there is a general southwards movement in the late summer: 100% of sightings in May have a northerly component in their direction of travel; by July, 65% of sightings have a southerly component.

these itinerant males that are seen in British waters, although their preference for deep water means that most sightings are at sea and not from land.

The distinctive angled blow appears first …

… then the head, back and dorsal hump slowly emerge; the whale may remain in this profile for some time, either resting motionless or travelling very slowly …

IDENTIFICATION:

The Sperm Whale is the largest of the toothed whales: mature males average about 15 m in length, and females about 10 m. The body is robust with wrinkled skin that is normally slate-grey or brown. The head is massive and blunt-ended, and comprises almost one-third of the animal's total length. The lower jaw is long, narrow and inconspicuous beneath the head.

DIVE SEQUENCE: Sperm Whales typically rest for long periods between dives, blowing infrequently as they log. Prior to a deep dive, typically lasting 25–90 minutes, the back is arched and the flukes raised as the animal dives vertically.

There is no dorsal fin, only a small triangular or rounded hump behind which there can be a series of 'knuckles' running down to the tail.

The distinctive blow is sideways, low and forward-angled due to the offset position of the blowhole.

The single blowhole is located to the left side of the front of the head.

The flukes, which are generally raised vertically prior to a deep dive, are large, broad and triangular with smooth edges and a deep central notch.

SIMILAR SPECIES: Sperm Whale overlaps in size with the largest whales. Like Humpback Whale (*page 66*) and the very rare Blue (*page 108*) and North Atlantic Right Whales (*page 109*), it raises its flukes before a deep dive. However, Sperm Whale's offset blow and surface profile should easily distinguish it from other large whales.

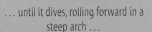

... until it dives, rolling forward in a steep arch ...

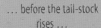

... before the tail-stock rises ...

... and the animal lifts its flukes vertically as it starts its dive.

Northern Bottlenose Whale

Hyperoodon ampullatus

Adult length:	7–9 m
Group size:	1–10
Breaching:	Occasional; leaps clear of water
Deep dive:	Tail flukes not raised
Blow:	Low and bushy, 1–2 m high; slightly angled forwards – usually visible in good conditions

BEHAVIOUR: Northern Bottlenose Whales are generally encountered logging or in slow-moving pods. They feed predominantly on squid which they hunt during dives that can last for over an hour. After such exertion animals may remain on the surface for 10 minutes or more at a time, blowing approximately every 30 seconds. Breaching and lob-tailing have been observed occasionally.

STATUS AND DISTRIBUTION:
Northern Bottlenose Whales are restricted to the North Atlantic, from the Caribbean and the Canaries north to West Greenland and Svalbard, with a preference for deep water (greater than 1,000 m) often over submarine canyons or adjacent to the continental shelf edge. This distribution correlates well with the habitat of squid of the genus *Gonatus*, which are its primary prey. That said, the species very occasionally enters waters of less than 300 m in depth, and has been subject to occasional stranding on the east coast of Britain, most notably the animal that received extensive media coverage when it swam up the River Thames in 2006.

OBSERVATION TIPS:
While exclusively (when in good health) a deepwater species, a chance encounter with a Northern Bottlenose Whale at sea may be amply rewarded as they are curious animals which readily approach stationary boats.

In north European waters the species occurs mainly in the months March–October, with a peak in sightings from northern Scotland in July–September. Sightings have increased in recent years in British and Irish waters, but the species remains rarely seen in happy circumstances.

The distinctive bulbous melon appears first (sometimes at a steep enough angle to reveal the beak), with the blow visible in calm conditions …

… then the back and dorsal fin, with the top of the head usually still visible …

IDENTIFICATION:

The Northern Bottlenose Whale is the largest beaked whale in the region, although it can only be reliably identified by the large, bulbous head which is usually best seen when a travelling animal breaks surface.

At close range, the rounded forehead can be seen to slightly overhang the short, protruding beak. Mature individuals often have a paler head.

A Northern Bottlenose Whale rolls to dive.

Northern Bottlenose Whale is a medium-sized whale, uniform grey to brown in colour on the upperparts, and creamy or pale-grey on the underside. It has a reasonably small, falcate dorsal fin situated two-thirds along the back.

SIMILAR SPECIES: Head-shape separates Northern Bottlenose Whale from both the similar Cuvier's Beaked Whale (*page 98*) and Minke Whale (*page 62*), neither of which has Northern Bottlenose's bulbous profile. Pod sizes of greater than two largely rule out Minke Whale – see *inside back cover*.

... and then the animal rolls languidly ...   ... before submerging with the tail-stock slightly arched.

Cuvier's Beaked Whale

Ziphius cavirostris

Adult length:	5–7 m
Group size:	1–12
Breaching:	rarely; almost vertically
Deep dive:	Tail flukes not raised
Blow:	Low and bushy, slightly angled forwards

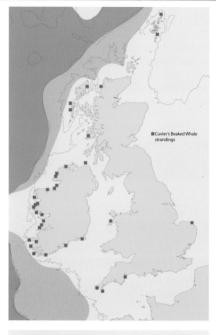

■Cuvier's Beaked Whale strandings

BEHAVIOUR: In recent years a fascinating picture has begun to emerge of the life history and habits of this hitherto poorly known whale. It seems that male Cuvier's Beaked Whales use their protruding teeth to fight each other in order to gain mating access to groups of mature females. Sightings of groups comprising exclusively females with calves suggest that the agressive males are given a wide berth. Animals have been recorded many times from the ferries operating in the Bay of Biscay, often surfacing very close-by and moving slowly within close proximity to the ship, indicating that they are an inquisitive species.

Cuvier's Beaked Whales rarely breach, but when they do they exit the water vertically before falling back in an ungainly manner. They feed primarily on deep water squid, though fish such as whiting are also taken.

OBSERVATION TIPS:
The most likely place to see a Cuvier's Beaked Whale in British waters is at sea in the Southwest Approaches, as this is closest to the species' stronghold in the Bay of Biscay.

STATUS AND DISTRIBUTION:

Cuvier's Beaked Whale has a worldwide distribution, generally in tropical and warm temperate seas and appearing to favour continental shelf slopes of 500–3,000 m depth.

Sightings from British waters show a clear westerly bias, with reports from the Southwest Approaches to the English Channel and as far north as the Western Isles in Scotland. While strandings have occurred in most months of the year, sightings at sea are mainly during May–September.

Although seen regularly further south in the Bay of Biscay, sightings from British waters remain extremely scarce, and most records relate to strandings.

The melon and head appear first (sometimes at a steep enough angle to reveal the beak) with the blow sometimes visible in calm conditions …

… then the back and dorsal fin, with the top of the head usually still visible …

IDENTIFICATION:

The Cuvier's Beaked Whale is one of the largest and most robust of the beaked whales and is best identified by a combination of its size, colouration/scarring and head-shape. Mature males develop a pair of teeth that protrude upwards from the tip of the lower jaw; mature females and immature animals of both sexes lack these protruding teeth.

The shape of the head and beak has been described as being like that of a goose, the forehead sloping gently to the tip of the short but distinct beak.

While young calves have all-dark bodies, immature animals generally develop pale heads and, with age, this paleness may extend along the back as far as the dorsal fin. Mature animals vary in colour from grey-brown to brown and have a longish back with a small, falcate dorsal fin situated two-thirds along the back.

The upper body is often heavily scarred in mature males, whilst females generally show little or no scarring.

SIMILAR SPECIES: Cuvier's Beaked Whale is similar in size and shape to other beaked whales, and also to Minke Whale (*page 62*) – but the distinctive head-shape distinguishes it from these species. Without the head-shape and pale colouration being seen, Cuvier's Beaked Whale cannot be reliably identified.

... and then the animal rolls languidly ...

... and submerges with the tail-stock slightly arched.

Mesoplodon Beaked Whales

Data Deficient

Four species of *Mesoplodon* beaked whale have been recorded in the European Atlantic; three in British waters, and a fourth, True's Beaked Whale, in Ireland.

The *Mesoplodon* species represent some of the rarest and most enigmatic of all the cetaceans. Squid-feeding denizens of deep, offshore waters, they are unobtrusive and inconspicuous, even when surfacing. Very little is known about their social behaviour, although they have been observed breaching (often multiple times), tail-slapping and porpoising.

There are very few records of *Mesoplodon* beaked whales from Britain, and most of these unfortunately relate to strandings. Some measure of their rarity to date is indicated by the fact that two of the species, Gervais' and Blainville's Beaked Whales, exist on the British cetacean list solely on the basis of single confirmed records – the former species as long ago as 1840! Sowerby's Beaked Whale appears to be the most common, on the basis of relatively regular sightings in the Faeroes Channel and the Bay of Biscay as well as the number of stranded animals recorded around the coastline of Britain and Ireland.

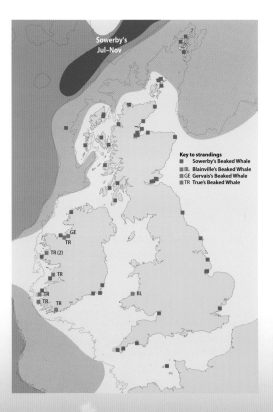

Sowerby's
Jul–Nov

Key to strandings
- Sowerby's Beaked Whale
- BL Blainville's Beaked Whale
- GE Gervais's Beaked Whale
- TR True's Beaked Whale

OBSERVATION TIPS:

The best chance of seeing one of these near-mythical whales must be at sea near or off the continental shelf. The regular ferry routes from the south coast of England down through the Bay of Biscay to Spain offer the best odds of encountering a *Mesoplodon*. By nature shy and retiring animals, merely chancing upon one of these species is hard enough; identifying them is quite another challenge. Relatively little is known about their behaviour at sea, and photographic material for them is poor compared to all other cetacean species.

If you are lucky enough to chance upon a beaked whale, having a camera to hand is likely to be key identifying it to species level. Adult males have distinctive and diagnostic protuberant teeth that aid identification – females and immatures, on the other hand, may be impossible to identify at sea.

The melon and head appear first (sometimes at a steep enough angle to reveal the beak) with the blow visible in calm conditions ...

... then the back ahead of the dorsal fin, with the top of the head usually still visible ...

Sowerby's Beaked Whale
Mesoplodon bidens

Adult length:	4·0–5·5 m
Group size:	1–8
Breaching:	Leaps almost vertically
Blow:	Small, bushy, forward

STATUS AND DISTRIBUTION:

The distribution of Sowerby's Beaked Whale appears to be centred upon deep water offshore water in the North Atlantic. With such a northerly bias to its distribution, it comes as little surprise that many of the European records of the species come from British and Irish waters. However, in common with the other *Mesoplodon* beaked whales, the majority of confirmed records are strandings.

Sightings of the Sowerby's Beaked Whale are rare but have occurred at sea as far north as the south of Iceland. In the UK, the range of the species has a westerly bias with records from the Southwest Approaches north to the Northern Isles. There have been exceptional strandings on beaches on the east coast of Britain, so, in common with many vagrant animals, the unexpected can and very occasionally does happen.

IDENTIFICATION: A small, slim whale which, like all *Mesoplodon* species, is reminiscent of an elongated dolphin in shape with a small, falcate dorsal fin located two-thirds of the way along the back. The upperparts are uniformly brown to grey, becoming paler towards the belly; the eyes are often encircled by a dark patch. The rounded forehead tapers to a slender beak, the length of which, although variable, is longer than in the other beaked whales. The long beak is reasonably distinctive when, as is often the case, it breaks the water at a steep angle as the animal surfaces. However, the only known diagnostic feature for identifying this species at sea is the two flattened teeth that protrude mid-way along the lower jaw in adult males (see *page 103*).

... and then the animal rolls smoothly ...

... and submerges with the tail-stock slightly arched.

True's Beaked Whale
Mesoplodon mirus

Adult length:	4·0–6·0 m
Group size:	1–6
Breaching:	Leaps almost vertically
Blow:	Unknown

STATUS AND DISTRIBUTION:
True's Beaked Whale remains one of the most enigmatic of the *Mesoplodon* beaked whales, and European records are predominantly of strandings. Of these, the majority have been from the west of Ireland, occurring on dates year-round, with six records prior to 1980 and four since, including 2 records from Killadoon, where a 4·59 m male stranded in February 1983 and a 5·4 m male stranded in November 1987. The 1997 record was of a female that live-stranded.

Confirmed strandings post 1980:
1983: *Killadoon, Co. Mayo, Ireland (Feb).*
1987: *Killadoon, Co. Mayo, Ireland (Nov).*
1997: *Ownahincha, Co. Cork, Ireland (Jun).*
2009: *Strandhill, Co. Sligo, Ireland (Mar).*

IDENTIFICATION: Typical *Mesoplodon* beaked whale shape. The head in front of the blowhole is distinctly bulbous, with a dark patch around the eye and a short, stubby beak. In adult males, a pair of teeth protrude from the tip of the lower jaw. The back is grey, though some individuals may show a darker spinal line and dorsal fin. The dorsal fin, which may appear falcate to triangular, is situated two-thirds of the way along the back.

Blainville's Beaked Whale
Mesoplodon densirostris

Adult length:	4·0–5·5 m
Group size:	1–6
Breaching:	Unknown
Blow:	Small, bushy, forward

STATUS AND DISTRIBUTION:
Blainville's Beaked Whale is perhaps the most widely distributed *Mesoplodon* species, found throughout the world's oceans apart from the Arctic, though it shows a preference for warm temperate and tropical waters. In the eastern North Atlantic, it is recorded comparatively regularly from Madeira and the Canaries. It is extremely rare elsewhere in the eastern North Atlantic; the sole British record was a stranding at Aberaeron on the coast of west Wales on 18 July 1993. In April 2005 a female stranded on the Dutch North Sea coast at Ameland in the West Frisian Islands.

IDENTIFICATION: Blainville's Beaked Whale is similar in size and shape to the other *Mesoplodon* beaked whales, with a small, falcate to triangular dorsal fin, a flattish head, and uniform grey or brown colouration on the body. Mature animals can be identified at sea by the unique shape of the beak, although seeing this at sea requires an exceptionally good encounter. The lower jaw is relatively short and distinctly arched, giving the impression, at a distance, of a bump on the forehead. In mature males, the arch is capped by two large, protruding teeth which are often encrusted in barnacles.

Gervais' Beaked Whale
Mesoplodon europaeus

Adult length:	4·6–6·0 m
Group size:	Unknown
Breaching:	Unknown
Blow:	Unknown

STATUS AND DISTRIBUTION: Gervais' Beaked Whale appears to be a mainly south-western North Atlantic species. There are only a handful of records of the species in the eastern North Atlantic, and just one record from British waters – the first known specimen, found floating in the English Channel in 1840. There is a single record from Ireland – an animal stranded on 22nd January 1989 at Ballysadare Bay, Co. Sligo.

IDENTIFICATION: Gervais' Beaked Whale is almost completely unknown at sea. It is known to have a typical *Mesoplodon* body shape with a small, falcate to triangular dorsal fin. The upperparts are dark grey, fading to paler below and the eye is often encircled by a dark patch. On surfacing, the beak is raised distinctly out of the water, when the small forehead that curves gently down to a shortish, slender beak may be seen. However, the only diagnostic feature at sea is the pair of teeth that emerge along the lower jaw one-third of the way from the tip in males.

BEAKED WHALES: Heads and beaks

TRUE'S BEAKED WHALE (male)
FOREHEAD: Round taper to a short, stubby beak. TEETH: At tip of lower jaw. COLOURATION: One source image shows a dark-tipped beak and virtually all-dark body, a second source image shows an individual with dark/light pattern similar to Gervais' Beaked Whale.

SOWERBY'S BEAKED WHALE (male)
FOREHEAD: Roundish taper to a long, slender beak. TEETH: Midway along lower jaw. COLOURATION: Sources show animals ranging from individuals with typical dark/light pattern to some with all-dark bodies and beaks ranging from dark-tipped to all-dark.

BLAINVILLE'S BEAKED WHALE (male)
FOREHEAD: Raised, arched jawline. TEETH: Irrupt from arching lower jaw. COLOURATION: Sources show some animals with dark/light pattern, others with all-dark bodies and beaks ranging from dark-tipped to all-dark.

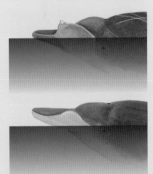

GERVAIS' BEAKED WHALE (male)
FOREHEAD: Smooth taper to a shortish, slender beak. TEETH: one-third distance from tip of lower jaw. COLOURATION: References (3 images) show a consistent light/dark pattern.

SOWERBY'S BEAKED WHALE (female)
FOREHEAD: Flatter taper than male to a long, slender beak. TEETH: None. COLOURATION: References show animals with classic *Mesoplodon* dark/light pattern and dark eye.

BLAINVILLE'S BEAKED WHALE (female)
FOREHEAD: Raised jawline. TEETH: None. COLOURATION: References show animals with either brown or grey bodies, and white or all-brown lower jaws.

IMPORTANT NOTE: The lack of confirmed sightings of *Mesoplodon* beaked whales means that there is little reference material on which to base illustrations. The illustrations shown here and on *page 90* are based on limited photographic and video footage – see *page 124*.

Striped Dolphin

Stenella coeruleoalba

Adult length:	1·8–2·5 m
Group size:	Generally 10–500
Behaviour:	Very active and more acrobatic than Common Dolphin; often cautious around boats, swimming in tightly packed pods

Jul–Sep

BEHAVIOUR: Striped Dolphins are highly social and acrobatic; usually seen in tight pods of about 25 animals, leaping, spinning and somersaulting clear of the water as they travel. This species is regularly seen in association with feeding Fin Whales, sometimes riding the bow-wave of a surfacing whale. Striped Dolphins feed on fish, such as sprat, Blue Whiting and anchovy, as well as small squid and crustaceans. They are usually cautious around moving vessels, swimming slowly in a tight group, but once the vessel has passed they may well move at speed and leap acrobatically in the wake. Striped Dolphins may form mixed-species groups with Short-beaked Common Dolphins.

STATUS AND DISTRIBUTION:

Striped Dolphins have a worldwide distribution, occurring in tropical, subtropical and warm temperate seas, with a preference for deep water beyond the continental shelf – rarely straying into shallower shelf waters. Although abundant in the European Atlantic, sightings from British waters remain localised, with records mainly from the Western Approaches and the Celtic Sea. There have been very rare sightings further north, including from Shetland.

However, there has been an increase in sightings of Striped Dolphins from the north European

OBSERVATION TIPS:
The best chance of seeing Striped Dolphin in British waters is to find some associating with feeding Fin Whales; a late summer pelagic trip out into the Western Approaches represents the best bet for finding both species at the same time.

continental shelf since 1990, which is believed to reflect an extension of warm oceanic currents and a corresponding rise in average sea temperatures. As this rising temperature trend is also reflected in British waters, it is possible that Striped Dolphins may be recorded with increasing frequency around the UK in the future.

IDENTIFICATION:

The Striped Dolphin is slender and streamlined with a distinctive flank pattern. It has a dark, prominent beak, gently sloping forehead and triangular dorsal fin that is slightly hooked.

The upperparts are dark grey, with a distinctive pale grey blaze that sweeps from the fore-flank back and up towards the dorsal fin. The pale grey flanks and the white or pinkish underparts are bisected by a thin, dark stripe that runs along the lower flanks from the eye to the underside of the tail-stock. Below this a second, shorter thin dark stripe runs back and down from the eye to above the flippers. However, these stripes can be difficult to see unless the dolphin jumps clear of the surface.

SIMILAR SPECIES: In poor light, or at long range, Striped Dolphin can be quite difficult to distinguish from Short-beaked Common Dolphin (*page 74*). Both species are broadly similar in size and shape and cannot be separated unless the distinctive flank patterning is seen. Confusion with the extremely rare Fraser's Dolphin (*page 116*) is also possible.

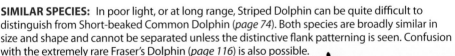

A travelling pod of Striped Dolphins is usually very active, tightly packed and with some individuals breaching, somersaulting and leaping up to 7 m above the surface. At a distance, the compact nature of the group, and variable height of the splashes, is a good indicator of this species. 105

A number of cetacean species have occurred in British waters just a handful of times. Some of these, like Blue and North Atlantic Right Whales were once much more relatively abundant than they are now, their current depauperate populations being a legacy of the impact of the early 20th century whaling industry. Although numbers of these animals may be slowly increasing, the recovery of such long-lived animals with low reproduction rates is inevitably a prolonged and incremental process. For this reason, such species should not expect to be seen in anything but the most exceptionally fortunate circumstances.

Other species, like the *Kogia* sperm whales, are exclusively deep water species and occur in British waters at the very limit of their range. They are therefore either rare or extremely unobtrusive (or both) and sightings are few and far between.

The sole British record to date of Fraser's Dolphin may offer a clue as to what we might expect to occur in the not too distant future. In recent years a general warming of British waters, possibly related to apparent changes in the global climate, have resulted in fish species that usually occur in the Mediterranean being found around the British coast. Fraser's Dolphin is normally associated with warm equatorial waters, so the British record may point to the vagrancy potential of cetaceans as a whole, or the potential for warm water species to occur further north as water temperatures increase. It may not be too long before the first confirmed sightings in British waters of live Melon-headed or Pygmy Killer Whales, or Rough-toothed Dolphin – all of which have been recorded relatively close by. In the meantime, many would settle for a long overdue repeat visit of a vagrant Narwhal….

Though not recorded alive in British waters yet, this True's Beaked Whale was seen in the nearby Bay of Biscay, where it breached an incredible 24 times, allowing a rare opportunity for an at-sea photograph of a live animal.

See also *Regularly occurring cetaceans page 60* and *Deepwater cetaceans page 90*

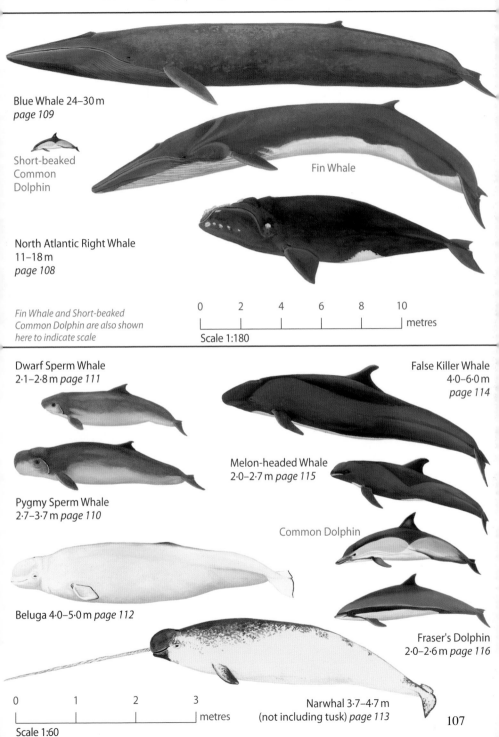

Blue Whale 24–30 m
page 109

Short-beaked
Common
Dolphin

Fin Whale

North Atlantic Right Whale
11–18 m
page 108

*Fin Whale and Short-beaked
Common Dolphin are also shown
here to indicate scale*

0	2	4	6	8	10

metres

Scale 1:180

Dwarf Sperm Whale
2·1–2·8 m *page 111*

False Killer Whale
4·0–6·0 m
page 114

Melon-headed Whale
2·0–2·7 m *page 115*

Pygmy Sperm Whale
2·7–3·7 m *page 110*

Common Dolphin

Beluga 4·0–5·0 m *page 112*

Fraser's Dolphin
2·0–2·6 m *page 116*

0	1	2	3

metres

Narwhal 3·7–4·7 m
(not including tusk) *page 113*

Scale 1:60

107

North Atlantic Right Whale
Eubalaena glacialis

Endangered	
Adult length:	11–18 m
Group size:	1–3, sometimes more
Breaching:	Often
Deep dive:	Usually raises tail flukes
Blow:	Distinctive, high, 'V'-shaped when viewed from front or rear

STATUS AND DISTRIBUTION: The North Atlantic Right Whale is probably the most endangered whale on earth, with an estimated population of about 350 animals. Its current range is a narrow band of the eastern seaboard of North America between Canada and Florida. The European population was once widespread, ranging from Spain to Norway and Iceland during the summer, and thought to spend the winter in its breeding grounds off West Africa. Once abundant in the Bay of Biscay, it was named *Eubalaena biscayensis* by early taxonomists.

Sadly, it is now considered all but extinct in European waters due to extensive whaling. Since 1980 there have been 2 documented sightings in British waters, and these, plus others off Iceland, Norway and in former breeding areas off the Canaries and Azores, may offer some hope that animals from the slowly increasing western population are spreading back into the eastern Atlantic.

Confirmed sightings post 1980:
2000: northwest of Rockall (Jun); north of Shetland (Jul).

IDENTIFICATION: The entirely black North Atlantic Right Whale is unmistakable. Its 'V'-shaped blow; broad, flat back lacking a dorsal fin; and characteristic pale lumps (or callosities) on the top of the huge head are diagnostic. These callosities, are above the eyes, along the lower jaw and around the rostrum and blowholes. The tail flukes, which are often raised on sounding, are very large, with smooth edges, pointed tips and a deep central notch.

The distinctively calloused head and blow ('V'-shaped unless seen from the side) appear together first ...

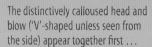

... followed by the back, with the top of the head and often part of the jawline still visible ...

... until the animal rolls, and the lack of a dorsal fin becomes apparent. This sequence is repeated ...

... unless diving, when the flukes appear.

Blue Whale
Balaenoptera musculus

Endangered	
Adult length:	24–30 m
Group size:	1–2, sometimes more
Breaching:	Occasionally young animals partially breach at a 45° angle or less
Deep dive:	Often raises tail flukes
Blow:	Massive, dense column up to 10 m high

STATUS AND DISTRIBUTION: Blue Whales have a worldwide distribution, are globally threatened, and are considered very rare in the eastern North Atlantic. It occurs in deep waters south from Iceland and Svalbard to the waters off the Iberian Peninsula. The species is extremely rare in British and Irish waters, and while recorded acoustically year-round (particularly in November and December) with SOSUS hydrophone arrays to the north and west of Britain and Ireland, sightings are incredibly rare and way out at sea. These few sightings have been during May–September, coinciding with the time that hydrophone recordings show an increase in the species' activity towards a late autumn/ early winter peak after the quietest time in March–June.

IDENTIFICATION: Typically, the massive blow, which can be 10 m high, is the first indication of the presence of a Blue Whale. The huge, blue-grey mottled body of a travelling whale stays low in the water. At a distance, or in poor light Blue Whales can appear dark, like a Fin Whale (*page 64*), but the prominent splashguard in front of the blowhole and the tiny dorsal fin located slightly more than two-thirds of the way along the back are distinctive.

The huge blow appears first ...

... then, slowly, the first part of the back (being so large an animal the dorsal fin is still below surface) ...

... before the animal rolls revealing most of the tail-stock and repeats the sequence ...

... unless it enters a deep dive when often the flukes appear.

Pygmy Sperm Whale
Kogia breviceps

Data Deficient	
Adult length:	2·7–3·7 m
Group size:	1–6
Breaching:	Occasional; vertical
Deep dive:	Sinks below surface
Blow:	Low, very light; blowhole offset slightly to the left

STATUS AND DISTRIBUTION:

The global distribution of the squid-eating Pygmy Sperm Whale is not well known. It may be fairly common, but just rarely encountered due to its size and behaviour. The information collected from strandings, together with a few sightings at sea, indicate that it occurs worldwide, favouring the deep waters of tropical, subtropical and temperate oceans. The species is believed to occur regularly, and is possibly resident, in the deeper waters of the Bay of Biscay, the Southwest Approaches and west of Ireland. Since 1980, there have been just two live sightings and over a dozen strandings in Britain. The strandings from Pembrokeshire in 1997 and Stranraer in 1999 being notable as they were live strandings, the latter involving a mother and calf. The live sighting from Shetland involved an injured animal at sea which washed up dead a week or so later.

Confirmed sightings and *strandings* post 1980:

1982: Off NW Ireland (Jun).
1985: *Barna, Co. Galway, Ireland (Oct).*
1993: *Nr Lynmouth, Devon (Oct).*
1997: *Lundy, Devon (Jan); Manorbier, Pembrokeshire (Oct).* **1998**: *Clew Bay, Co. Mayo, Ireland (–).* **1999**: *Murrisk, Co. Mayo, Ireland (Jul); Stranraer, Dumfries and Galloway (Oct).* **2000**: *Killeeneran, Co. Galway, Ireland (Jun).* **2002**: *Thurlestone, Devon (Jan); Castlegregory, Co. Kerry, Ireland (Jul).* **2005**: *Ballyheigue, Co. Kerry, Ireland (Nov).* **2007**: Mainland, Shetland (Oct). **2009**: *Nr Sneem, Co. Kerry, Ireland (Jan); Dungarvan, Co. Waterford, Ireland (Jan).* **2011**: *Isle of Seil, Argyll and Bute (Oct).*

IDENTIFICATION: Due to its size, the first impression of a Pygmy Sperm Whale may be that of a dolphin or a porpoise. However, its structure and behaviour make it quite unlike either. Pygmy Sperm Whales are compact animals with a blunt, squarish head and a robust body with a very small hook-shaped dorsal fin located just over halfway along the back. They are soft blue-grey above and cream to pinkish-grey underneath. They are typically encountered logging motionless at the surface or travelling in a series of shallow lethargic rolls. They do not tend to dive, but instead sink slowly below the surface.

Pygmy Sperm Whale has a small, falcate, dorsal fin located more than halfway along the back.

Dwarf Sperm Whale has a relatively broad-based dorsal fin that is located centrally on the back .

Pygmy and Dwarf Sperm Whales are almost identical and a good view or series of photographs is needed to confirm identification. Due to their lethargic and inconspicuous nature they are rarely seen at sea, and even then usually only in very calm conditions.

Dwarf Sperm Whale
Kogia sima

Data Deficient	
Adult length:	2·1–2·8 m
Group size:	1–10
Breaching:	Occasional; vertical
Deep dive:	Sinks below surface
Blow:	Low, very light; blowhole offset slightly to the left

STATUS AND DISTRIBUTION: The few records of Dwarf Sperm Whale indicate that it is widely distributed in tropical, subtropical and temperate seas, and favours deep water near the edge of continental shelves. The lack of sightings or stranding records from the north-east Atlantic suggest that the species is genuinely rare. One animal stranded in France, on the south Brittany coast, in October 1991. There is one confirmed sighting in British waters, in Mount's Bay, Cornwall in October 2011.

IDENTIFICATION: The Dwarf Sperm Whale is almost identical to the Pygmy Sperm Whale in colour and form and telling them apart is a challenge. Dwarf is slightly smaller than Pygmy; the head is less blunt and the dorsal fin, though variable in shape and size, is broader-based and located centrally on the back.

Dwarf Sperm Whale

Pygmy Sperm Whale

Beluga *Delphinapterus leucas*

Near Threatened	
Adult length:	4–5 m
Group size:	2–10; same gender groups common
Breaching:	Rare
Deep dive:	Tail flukes sometimes break surface at a low angle
Blow:	Low and inconspicuous

STATUS AND DISTRIBUTION: The Beluga has a circumpolar distribution and occurs in Arctic and sub-Arctic waters. On the eastern side of the Atlantic, the species is found in the Barents and Greenland Seas. During the summer months following the retreat of winter sea-ice, Beluga are found in shallow northern bays around the islands of Jan Mayen, Novoya Zemlya, Svalbard and Bear Island; during the winter it moves further south, including off the coast of Scandinavia, and occasionally reaches the northern North Sea. The species is therefore extremely rare in British and Irish waters, with just 16 records since 1900. Of the six sightings since 1980, three were in 1988.

There is a perhaps expected northerly and eastern bias to the records given the species' origins.

Confirmed sightings post 1980:
1987: Scarborough and Whitby, Yorkshire (Jun). **1988**: Hadston, Northumberland (Mar); Cork Harbour, Co. Cork, Ireland (Jun); Balintore, Ross and Cromarty (Jun). **1995**: Loch Duich and Applecross, Highland (Apr). **1996**: Mainland, Shetland (Sep). **1997**: Unst, Shetland (Aug).

IDENTIFICATION: A stout, muscular, all-white body and absence of a dorsal fin makes a mature Beluga unmistakable. The rounded head is small in relation to the body and has a prominent bulbous melon above a short beak. Belugas also have a narrow dorsal ridge along the rear half of the back. At birth they are uniformly dark, becoming paler as they age, taking 7–9 years before attaining the pure white skin of a mature animal, and even then the dorsal ridge and the edges of the flippers and flukes may remain dark. Belugas are sluggish swimmers but are inquisitive and active, often spy-hopping and tail-slapping.

Narwhal *Monodon monoceros*

Near Threatened	
Adult length:	4–5 m (not including tusk of up to 3 m)
Group size:	Family groups of 2–20 in summer; more solitary in winter
Breaching:	Acrobatic but seldom breaches fully
Deep dive:	Tail flukes not raised
Blow:	Low and inconspicuous

STATUS AND DISTRIBUTION: Narwhal has a discontinuous circumpolar range, mostly from the Arctic Circle to the north to the edge of the icecap; they rarely occur further south than 70° N. Narwhal feed on a specialised diet of halibut, cod and medium-sized (25–40 cm) squid.

There have been no confirmed strandings or sightings in Britain since 1949, when 4 individuals were recorded. In the first half of the 20th Century there were a number of confirmed records, not only as might be expected from the Northern Isles, but also as far south as Essex and Kent.

IDENTIFICATION: Adult male Narwhals are unlikely to be confused with any other species, possessing, as they do, a long (up to 3 m) spiralling tusk that protrudes from their upper jaw. The body is stout, with a small hump instead of a dorsal fin. The head is proportionally rather small, with a pronounced, round melon. The back and sides are marbled grey and the belly is much paler or white.

False Killer Whale
Pseudorca crassidens

Adult length:	4–6 m
Group size:	2–200
Breaching:	Frequent
Blow:	Small, bushy; inconspicuous

STATUS AND DISTRIBUTION:
The False Killer Whale is a deep ocean, predominantly squid-feeding species found in tropical and warm temperate waters. It is thinly distributed throughout its wide range, the northern limit of which appears to be around the Straits of Gibraltar. It has, however, been recorded in British waters, with mass strandings in 1927, 1934 and 1935. Since 1976, there have been five sightings at sea, ranging from the Southwest Approaches to as far north as Orkney, where a pod of between 100 and 150 animals was seen 50 km east of the archipelago in July 1981. Four of these five sightings have been in July or August. The occurrence of the

False Killer Whale north of its normal range is almost certainly linked to the periodic incursion of warm water into the region.

Confirmed sightings post 1980:
1980: At sea, SW Approaches [2] (Aug).
1981: At sea, east of Orkney [100–150] (Jul).
1989: At sea, west of Isle of Skye, Highland (Aug).
1991: At sea, north-east of Aberdeen [10–20](Aug).

IDENTIFICATION: False Killer Whales are large, streamlined predators. The body is uniformly dark, the head is slender and tapering, and the dorsal fin is large, prominent and falcate, located centrally on the back. They are highly active, often seen in family groups travelling at speed with their heads and upper bodies above the surface.

Melon-headed Whale
Peponocephala electra

Adult length:	2·0–2·7 m
Group size:	up to 50+ in tropics
Breaching:	Occasional
Blow:	Low and inconspicuous

STATUS AND DISTRIBUTION:

An equatorial species that is rarely sighted in subtropical and warm temperate seas. The only British record relates to a skull found near Charlestown, Cornwall, in September 1949. A stranding near La Rochelle, France in 2003, a sighting off Brittany in 2011, and a number of other possible sightings (either of this species or Pygmy Killer Whale *Feresa attenuata*) from the Bay of Biscay in recent years point to the potential occurrence of this species in British waters.

IDENTIFICATION: Although Melon-headed Whales are dolphin-sized, they are actually blackfish and their all-dark colouration and lack of a protruding beak should rule out most dolphin species. Melon-headed Whales are fast-moving, with a relatively bulky body forward of the centrally located, falcate dorsal fin, tapering to a thin tail-stock at the rear. Although appearing dark grey overall at distance, a close view should enable a dark dorsal cape to be seen. This is widest below the dorsal fin and contrasts with the slightly paler flanks. In good light, the face of Melon-headed Whale appears darker than the flanks, giving the animal a masked appearance. A close view will reveal white lips and a white anchor-shaped throat patch and hindbelly. Melon-headed Whale has a relatively pointed (melon-shaped) head and sharply pointed flippers, which differentiate it from the very similar Pygmy Killer Whale, though these features can be difficult to observe at sea.

Fraser's Dolphin
Lagenodelphis hosei

Adult length:	2·0–2·6 m
Group size:	100–1,000 in tropics
Breaching:	Highly active; acrobatic

STATUS AND DISTRIBUTION: The status and distribution of Fraser's Dolphin is not well known. It can be found around the world, generally restricted to deep tropical waters between 30° S and 20° N. Considering that the species has only been sighted at sea as far north as the Azores and Madeira, the single British record of a stranded animal discovered on South Uist, Western Isles, Scotland in September 1996 is exceptional to say the least.

IDENTIFICATION: Fraser's Dolphin has a highly characteristic shape – small and stocky with a short but distinct beak and a relatively small flipper, flukes and dorsal fin. The dorsal fin is almost triangular and can appear to be angled slightly forwards in males. The patterning and colouration of the body are also distinctive – bluish-grey above and pinkish-white below with a thick, dark stripe that extends from the eye, often creating a masked appearance, along the flank to the anus. This stripe becomes wider and darker with age, being least well-defined in juveniles and most striking in adult males. A cream-coloured line runs from the forehead along the upper edge of the flank stripe and another dark stripe runs from the base of the lower jaw to the front of the flipper.

Threats and conservation

For a nation that prides itself upon its maritime history, our track record in marine conservation is somewhat chequered. In living memory, whales were still being hunted commercially in British waters, and it is not so long ago that the killing of seals for their skins was an accepted cottage industry in some parts of Britain. Whilst those days are now long gone, the marine mammals that live in or pass through our waters still face considerable challenges imposed upon them by our use of their natural habitat.

Preparing seal skins in the early 1960s at Skaw, Whalsay (Shetland).

The days of unregulated fishing may have passed, but there remains a considerable demand for fish from British waters. This has consequences for the marine life higher in the food chain, foremost amongst which are marine mammals. There is no single animal with a bigger impact upon marine food-stocks than man, and it would be naïve to think that our demand for fish does not directly compete with, and indeed out-compete other predators.

Our consumption of fish does not simply equate to competition with other animals; the means by which we take that resource from the sea may also have consequences for marine mammals. Whether it is the 360,000 cetaceans drowned in fishing nets as by-catch globally each year, or

A tangle of nylon and plastic at the high water mark – an all too common sight on the world's beaches.

injuries sustained by marine mammals through interactions with propellers or other fishing gear, the use of the sea by man is still not without serious implications for marine mammals.

Discarded or lost fishing gear is only a small part of the plethora of other man-made marine waste that is suspended in our waters – around 20,000 tonnes of marine litter is dumped annually into the North Sea alone. Plastic waste forms the bulk of this litter and can entangle or be ingested by marine wildlife; it is estimated that, globally, 100,000 marine mammals and 1,000,000 birds die annually as a result of interaction with discarded plastics in the marine environment. These are chilling statistics.

There is, however, some scope for cautious optimism. Growing interest and concern about the state of our seas, on the part of public bodies and the primary marine fishing industry, and amongst the general public, confirms that it is in everyone's best interest to ensure the marine environment is managed sustainably. Organisations such as Kommunenes Internasjonale Miljøorganisasjon (KIMO) represent this sea-change in attitudes – KIMO is an organisation formed from an international association of coastal local authorities devoted to tackling the issues of marine waste through diplomatic, research-based, and practical measures working with, amongst others, fishermen themselves. Meanwhile, charities such as the Sea Watch Foundation and the Whale and Dolphin Conservation Society (WDCS) champion the cause of cetaceans worldwide, and provide an excellent portal through which members of the public can get actively involved in cetacean conservation in the UK and beyond.

Researchers collecting Killer Whale biological samples for subsequent laboratory analysis.

In recent years public interest in, and support for wildlife has burgeoned. As consumers, we can all exert considerable leverage by demanding that our fish comes from sustainably managed fisheries. As individuals, there are opportunities to become directly involved in conservation either as a fundraiser or as a volunteer. Many cetacean conservation and research organisations are delighted to provide survey training, for example, and the power of public data gathering should not be underestimated.

Recording and getting involved

Records of marine mammal sightings help to build an increasingly comprehensive and accurate picture of the distribution and state of health of our marine wildlife. With the advent of relatively cheap and high quality digital photography, images of individual cetaceans can now be collated by researchers, allowing previously undreamed of opportunities to track the movements of specific animals around our coast. For example, particular animals may have distinctive scarring to their back or dorsal fin which may assist in securing an identification of the individual concerned. Hence, whenever possible observers should try to get photographs of the animals involved in a cetacean sighting. There is still so much to learn about the species in our waters, and the opportunities to contribute to our collective knowledge are limited only by the time (and good fortune!) individual observers can devote to looking for cetaceans. A list of research and recording organisations can be found on page 123.

This Killer Whale's fin shape and blaze markings are unique – enabling this individual to be tracked and identified from photographs.

Volunteers being trained in cetacean re-floating.

Stranded cetaceans and marine mammal rescue

Occasionally, cetaceans strand upon our shores, either dead or still alive. Similarly, injured seals may be encountered from time to time. Animals found under such circumstances should, if still alive, be reported immediately to marine mammal rescue groups such as British Divers Marine Life Rescue (BDMLR) (see *page 123*). With experienced intervention, there is always a possibility that a live-stranded cetacean or an injured seal can be successfully re-floated or rehabilitated. Even a dead cetacean can contribute significant information via post-mortem, such as cause of death, diet, *etc.*

What to do if you see a live beached animal
Seals: Not every seal on land is in need of rescue. Lying on one side and waving a flipper in the air, making a 'banana' shape and barking at people who get too close, or just dozing are natural behaviours and not a cause for concern. Tear stains beneath a seal's eyes are a good sign that they are well hydrated – seals lack the ducts that re-circulate tears and so they appear to 'cry' continuously. Pups are often left on the beach and their mothers will usually haul out to suckle them at high tide. It is important not to touch them as their mother may desert them.

Grey Seal pups are born in the autumn and winter and, although they may appear to be abandoned, do not enter the sea until they are 3–4 weeks old.

Common Seal pups, born from June to September, can swim within a few hours and may be in and out of the water regularly. Disease, parasitic infection, wounds and netting can be a problem and some seals may suffer from these. Pups may become separated from their mothers after a storm or spring tide and can become undernourished very quickly.

If you think a seal is ill or distressed, call BDMLR for advice and assistance. If you can send some photographs from your phone then they will give you a number or email address to send them to.

- Do not pick the seal up – observe it from a safe distance.
- Do not chase it back in the sea – try to stand between it and the sea until help arrives.
- Look for signs of injury and provide an accurate description of these to BDMLR and also the location, species (if known) and size.

- Keep other people and dogs away since they can cause stress to the animal. Seals also carry infections that can be transmitted.
- Avoid inhaling the seal's breath and avoid their head as they can inflict nasty bites.

Whales, dolphins or porpoises: A whale, dolphin or porpoise stranded on the beach is obviously not usual and they will require assistance.
If you see one on a beach, call BDMLR quickly and then give the animal basic first aid as follows:

- Do not put it back in the sea without advice from BDMLR or a vet. You may cause it additional and unnecessary suffering.
- Look for signs of injury and provide an accurate description of these, the size and species (if known) and location of the animal to BDMLR. If you can send some photographs from your mobile phone then they will give you a number or email address to send them to.
- If the animal is on its side, if it is small enough gently roll it upright and dig shallow trenches beneath its pectoral fins.
- Keep the skin wet to stop cracking and to keep the animal cool. Seaweed or wet sheets on its back will help. Pour water over it gently but do not allow any to enter the blowhole.
- Keep other people and dogs away since they can cause stress to the animal.
- Avoid inhaling the animal's breath and stay upwind if you are working close to the head.

If you find a dead cetacean
The Cetacean Strandings Investigation Programme (CSIP) collect data on each UK stranding and may be interested in carrying out a post-mortem. If you discover a dead stranded animal, please contact the CSIP hotline 0800 6520333 and give a description of the following where possible:

Location and date found; species and sex; overall length; condition of the animal; and your contact details should further information be needed.

Digital images are extremely helpful in the identification of stranded species, as well as ascertaining whether the body may be suitable for a post-mortem. If possible, please forward any images that may have been taken with a digital camera or phone.

Observation guidelines

Seals – on land

There are no formal, legally binding guidelines for viewing seals on land in Britain. They should be treated in the same way as when one watches any wild animals – with common-sense, respect for the animals' welfare at all times, and good field-craft.

Seals are sensitive to disturbance, and careless behaviour on the part of observers at their haul-out sites will result in them returning with haste to the security of the sea. This can have profound impacts upon the animals, such as a general loss of condition through the needless expenditure of energy. Interference with un-weaned young can reduce their health through disrupted feeding, or even lead to their loss or abandonment by their mothers. Ultimately, disturbance can lead to the abandonment of haul-out sites.

These consequences can be readily avoided by following these simple guidelines:

- Keep below the skyline, and minimise your profile – seals often associate the shape of a standing human being with danger. Observers should wear drab-coloured clothing, approach slowly, and use available cover (dunes, vegetation *etc.*) to conceal themselves. Where seals are hauled out close to a road, a vehicle makes an excellent hide from which to observe them.

- Keep noise to a minimum – seals have excellent hearing, and are alert to unexpected noises that may indicate a nearby threat.

- Be aware of progressive behavioural signs that indicate you are too close – you should proceed no closer once a seal becomes even slightly agitated, indicating it is aware of your presence. If seals begin to move back towards the sea, the observer is already too close, and should carefully retreat at once; once seals are entering water, the damage has already been done. This can of course happen inadvertently when seals are encountered unexpectedly; under these circumstances, the site should be left immediately so the animals can return without hindrance.

- Leave seal pups well alone – their mothers are often nearby, and may abandon their young if they witness an inappropriate approach. Be aware that seal pups are not as defenceless as their appearance might suggest – they can and will bite if threatened. (If bitten, medical assistance should be sought, as seal bites transmit some unpleasant bacteria.)

- Use binoculars and/or cameras to close the distance – excellent views of seals can be obtained using suitable optical aids.

- Avoid using flash photography – sudden bright lights can be frightening for all mammals.

Make the most of sites at which seals are more habituated to human activity, or suitable viewing arrangements are in place; such as Lerwick harbour or Donna Nook.

Sea vessels – at sea

There are no formal, legally binding guidelines for viewing cetaceans encountered whilst at sea in Britain. However, as these are sensitive and intelligent animals, there is potential for disturbance and distress to be caused if those observing them do not do so in an appropriate and respectful manner. The onus for behaving responsibly therefore rests upon the boat operators in question. Sea Watch Foundation provides a Marine Code of Conduct, as follows:

- If you sight dolphins at a distance, make forward progress maintaining a steady speed, slowing down to six knots or less when you are within a kilometre of them.

- Do not chase dolphins, drive a boat directly towards them or encircle them; wherever possible, let them approach you. If they choose to bow-ride, maintain a steady speed and course.

- Do not respond to them by changing course or speed in a sudden or erratic manner; slowing down or stopping suddenly can confuse and alarm dolphins as much as sudden acceleration.

- Allow groups of dolphins to remain together. Avoid deliberately driving through, or between, groups of cetaceans.

- Avoid close approach to dolphins with young. You risk disrupting mother-calf bonds and exposing inexperienced young to stress and possible boat strikes

- Do not swim with, touch or feed dolphins, for your safety and theirs. Besides the stress you can cause them, remember that, just as in humans, diseases can be spread by close contact, and dolphins

are larger than humans and can cause unwitting injury.

- Ensure that no more than two vessels are within a kilometre of dolphins at any one time and no more than one boat within close proximity. Refrain from calling other vessels to join you.

- Always allow dolphins an escape route. Avoid boxing them in between vessels.

- Move away slowly if you notice signs of disturbance, such as repeated avoidance behaviour, erratic changes in speed and direction, or lengthy periods underwater.

- Possible sources of noise disturbance can be avoided by ensuring speeds are never greater than ten knots, and by keeping the engine and propeller well maintained. On the other hand, care should be taken to avoid collision with dolphins when using sailing boats or boats with a low engine noise, as the animals are less likely to hear the vessel until it is close.

- People regularly using vessels in areas where dolphins are known to occur should consider fitting propeller guards to minimize the risk of injury to dolphins.

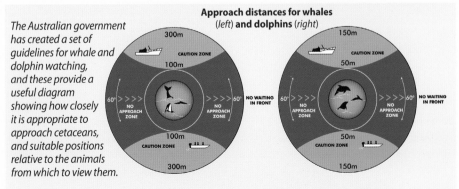

The Australian government has created a set of guidelines for whale and dolphin watching, and these provide a useful diagram showing how closely it is appropriate to approach cetaceans, and suitable positions relative to the animals from which to view them.

Approach distances for whales (*left*) **and dolphins** (*right*)

www.environment.gov.au/coasts/publications/pubs/whale-watching-guidelines-2005.pdf

Further reading

A guide to the identification of the Whales and Dolphins of Ireland. J. Wilson & S. Berrow. 2006. The Irish Whale and Dolphin Group (IWDG), Ireland.

A guide to the whales, dolphins and porpoises of the United Kingdom (2000). The first WDCS annual report on the status of UK cetaceans. D. Walker & M. De Boer. 2003. Whale and Dolphin Conservation Society (WDCS), UK.

A Guide to the Identification of Whales, Dolphins and Porpoises in European Seas. P.G.H. Evans. 1995. Scottish Natural Heritage, UK.

Abundance and behaviour of cetaceans and basking sharks in the Pentland Firth and Orkney Waters. P. G. H. Evans, M. E. Baines & J. Coppock. 2011. Hebog Environmental Ltd & Sea Watch Foundation. Scottish Natural Heritage Commissioned Report No. 419.

Atlas of Cetacean distribution in north-west European waters. J. B. Reid, P. G. H. Evans & S. P. Northridge. 2003. Joint Nature Conservation Committee.

Cetacean observations during seismic surveys in 1997. C. J. Stone. 1998. JNCC Reports No. 278.

Irish Cetacean Review (2000–2009). S. D. Berrow, P. Whooley, M. O'Connell & D. Wall. 2010. Irish Whale and Dolphin Group.

ORCA No 1. A Report on the Whales, Dolphins and Seabirds of the Bay of Biscay and the English Channel. G. Cresswell & D. Walker (Eds.). 2001. Organisation Cetacea (ORCA), UK.

ORCA No. 2. Incorporating a report on the whales, dolphins and seabirds of the Bay of Biscay and English Channel. G. Cresswell & D. Walker. 2002. Organisation Cetacea (ORCA), UK.

ORCA No. 3. The Annual Report of Organisation Cetacea. D. Walker (Ed.). 2004. Organisation Cetacea (ORCA), UK.

The Best Whale Watching In Europe. A guide to seeing whales, dolphins and porpoises in all European waters. E. Hoyt. 2003. Whale and Dolphin Conservation Society (WDCS), Unterhaching, Germany.

UK Cetacean Status Review. P. G. H. Evans, P. Anderwald & M. E. Baines. Sea Watch Foundation. 2003. Report to English Nature & Countryside Council for Wales.

Whales and Dolphins: Guide to the Biology and Behaviour of Cetaceans. M. Wuirtz & N. Repetto. 1998. Swan Hill Press, UK.

Whales and Dolphins in Shetland Waters. P.G.H. Evans. UK Mammal Society Cetacean Group. 1993. Shetland Cetacean Report.

Whales and Dolphins of Great Britain. D. Walker & A. Wilson. 2007. Cetacea Publishing.

Whales and Dolphins of the European Atlantic. D. Walker & G. Cresswell. 2008. Princeton WILDGuides.

Whales, Dolphins and Porpoises. M. Carwardine & M. Camm. 1995. Dorling Kindersley.

Whales, Dolphins and Seals. A Field Guide to the Marine Mammals of the World. H. Shirihai & B. Jarrett. 2006. A&C Black Publishers Ltd, London.

Useful addresses

CETACEAN RESCUE
British Divers Marine Life Rescue
www.bdmlr.org.uk
Lime House, Regency Close, Uckfield,
East Sussex TN22 1DS
BDMLR hotline: 01825 765546 (office
hours) or 07787 433412 (Bank holidays,
evenings and weekends)

British Divers Marine Life Rescue (BDMLR)
was formed in 1988, since when they have
been involved in the rescue of marine wildlife
after every major marine disaster and mass
stranding of cetaceans around the UK.
Seal rescue has remained a major component
of their work, with BDMLR medics rescuing
seals in all seasons. Over the years, many
hundreds of seals have been helped – with
BDMLR working closely with specialist
rehabilitation facilities to ensure their long-
term care and eventual return to the wild.
Although seal rescue remains a key part of
BDMLR's work, it has recently become more
involved with cetacean strandings.

Today, BDMLR attend over 450 incidents a year,
and since 1988 has trained over 8,500 people
to become volunteer Marine Mammal Medics.
The only marine animal rescue organisation
that covers England, Wales and Scotland, they
also train the RSPCA, SSPCA, Coastguard and
Police and maintain direct links with them.

BDMLR has rescue equipment located at
strategic points around the UK and about 2,500
medics on their database – all ready to assist
marine animals in distress.

UK Cetacean Strandings Investigation Programme
www.ukstrandings.org
CSIP hotline: 0800 6520333

EVENTS
WhaleFest
www.whale-fest.com
The world's biggest celebration of wild whales
and dolphins. The event attracts interest from
across the world, and is packed with trips, fun
family activities, celebrity speakers. And what's
more, it's the culmination of a whole week of
cetacean-themed music, arts and culture – all
supporting efforts to protect our oceans.

WHALE-WATCHING
Planet Whale
www.planetwhale.com
2A Church Road, Hove East Sussex BN3 2FL
Planet Whale is an online resource for whale
watching, with a searchable directory of
worldwide whale and dolphin watching tours.
Trips are reviewed by the public based on a
set of sustainability criteria, so users can easily
discover the most responsible tours in each
country. The site also hosts the largest directory
of whale and dolphin charities in existence,
with details of their campaigns, projects, and
volunteering opportunities.

WiSe Scheme
www.wisescheme.org

Promotes responsible wildlife-watching
through training, accreditation and
awareness-raising.

RECORDING AND RESEARCH
Irish Whale and Dolphin Group
www.iwdg.ie
Merchants Quay, Kilrush, County Clare

Marine Conservation Society
www.mcsuk.org
Unit 3, Wolf Business Park, Alton Road,
Ross-on-Wye, Herefordshire HR9 5NB

ORCA (Organisation Cetacea)
www.orcaweb.org.uk
Brittany Centre, Wharf Road, Portsmouth
PO2 8RU

Sea Mammal Research Unit
www.smru.st-andrews.ac.uk
Scottish Oceans Institute, University of
St Andrews, St Andrews, Fife KY16 8LB

Sea Watch Foundation
www.seawatchfoundation.org.uk
Ewyn y Don, Bull Bay, Anglesey LL68 9SD

Whale and Dolphin Conservation Society
www.wdcs.org
Brookfield House, 38 St. Paul Street,
Chippenham Wiltshire SN15 1LJ

Photographic and artwork credits

Front Cover **Common Seal**: Hugh Harrop.
p.1   **Killer Whales**: Hugh Harrop.
p.5   **Risso's Dolphins**: Jon Dunn.
p.8   **European Otter**: Hugh Harrop.
p.9   Common Seal: Rob Still.
p.11   Humpback Whale and
        Northern Bottlenose Whale: Rob Still.
p.12   **Fin Whale**: Hugh Harrop.
        Sperm Whale: Hugh Harrop.
p.13   **Cuvier's beaked Whale**: Hugh Harrop.
        Long-finned Pilot Whale: Hugh Harrop.
p.14   **Short-beaked Common Dolphins**:
        Hugh Harrop.
p.14   **Harbour Porpoise**: Hilary Chambers.
p.15   **Walrus**: Polar Cruises.
        Grey Seal: Hugh Harrop.
p.17   *Sea States 0–9*: Dylan Walker.
p.18   *Looking for marine mammals from land*:
        Hugh Harrop.
p.20   **Humpback Whale** and **White-beaked**
        Dolphin; *beside boat*: Dylan Walker.
        Risso's Dolphin: Hugh Harrop.
        Bottlenose Dolphin: Hugh Harrop.
p.21   **Bottlenose Dolphin**: CIRCE.
        Bottlenose Dolphin: CIRCE.
        Minke Whale: Dylan Walker.
        Sowerby's beaked Whale:
        Marina Milligan / Hal Whitehead Lab.
        Long-finned Pilot Whale: Dylan Walker.
        Short-beaked Common Dolphins:
        Dylan Walker.
        Fin Whale; *distant blow*: Hugh Harrop.
        Basking Shark: Hugh Harrop.
p.22   **Bottlenose Dolphin**; *bow-riding*:
        Alan Ward.
        Short-beaked Common Dolphin;
        porpoising: Stephen Marsh BDMLR.
p.23   **Fin Whale**; *blow*: Hugh Harrop.
        Humpback Whale; *fluking*: Dave Fletcher.
p.24   **Minke Whale**; *breaching*: Michael J. Tetley.
        Sei Whale; *lunge-feeding*:
        George Graham.
p.25   **Humpback Whale**; *lob-tailing*: A. Davey.
        Risso's Dolphin;
        tail-slapping; chorus line: Jon Dunn.
        Long-finned Pilot Whales;
        logging; spy-hopping: Hugh Harrop.
p.26   **Killer Whales**; *with wildlife-viewing boat*:
        John Bateson.
p.28   *Blakeney seals* (backdrop): Duncan Harris.
        Skomer: Mark Thomas Jones.
        Lerwick Harbour: Vicky Brock.
        Old Man of Hoy, Orkney: Hugh Harrop.

p.29   *Donna Nook*: Kev Chapman.
        Farne Islands: I. Hadwick.
        Blakeney: Freddie Phillips.
p.30   *Isles of Scilly* (backdrop): Michael Day.
p.31   *Cape Cornwall*: Shiro Shazan.
p.32   *Cardigan Bay* (backdrop): Graham Well.
p.33   *Ramsey Island*: Spike Harris.
        Strumble Head: Matthew Britton.
p.34   *Loop Head* (backdrop): Graham Churchard.
p.35   *Whale watching at Dunree*: Greg Clarke.
p.36   *Chanonry Point* (backdrop): Hugh Harrop.
p.37   *Girdleness*: Ian Cowe.
        Flamborough Head: Alan Harris.
p.38   *Mousa, Shetland* (backdrop): Hugh Harrop.
p.39   *Orkney Ferry*: Hugh Harrop.
p.40   *The Minch* (backdrop): Kyle Taylor.
p.41   *Tiumpan Head, Lewis*: Ian Windey.
p.42   **Grey Seal**: Hugh Harrop.

SEALS
p.45   **Common Seal**; *all images*: Hugh Harrop.
p.46   **Common Seal**; *all images*: Hugh Harrop.
p.47   **Common Seal**; *all images*: Hugh Harrop.
p.49   **Grey Seal**; *male; female; male in water*:
        Hugh Harrop.
        Grey Seal; *pup*: Kevin Chapman.
p.50   **Grey Seal**; *all images*: Hugh Harrop.
p.51   **Grey Seal**; *all images*: Hugh Harrop.
p.52   **Grey Seal** and **Common Seal**;
        all images: Hugh Harrop.
p.53   **Walrus**: Polar Cruises.
p.54   **Ringed Seal**: Frantz Vangen.
p.55   **Bearded Seal**: Jon Dunn.
p.56   **Harp Seal**: Tom Tams.
p.57   **Hooded Seal**: Bobby Tulloch.

CETACEANS – REGULARLY OCCURRING SPECIES
p.58   **Killer Whale**: Hugh Harrop.
p.60   All illustrations: Rob Still.
p.63   **Minke Whale**;
        roll dive; profile: Hugh Harrop.
        Minke Whale; *blow*: Graeme Creswell.
        Minke Whale; *first surface*: Mike Baird.
p.65   **Fin Whale**; *all images*: Hugh Harrop.
p.67   **Humpback Whale**;
        body arch; fluking: Hugh Harrop.
        Humpback Whale;
        surfacing and blowing: Virt Kitty.
        Humpback Whale; *pectoral fln*:
        Pat Hawks.
p.69   **Killer Whale**; *all images*: Hugh Harrop.
p.70   **Killer Whale**; *all images*: Hugh Harrop.
p.71   **Killer Whale**; *all images*: Hugh Harrop.

p.73 **Long-finned Pilot Whale;**
roll; spy hopping; female: Hugh Harrop.
Long-finned Pilot Whale;
male: Glenn Overington.

p.75 **Short-beaked Common Dolphin;**
all images: Hugh Harrop.

p.76 **Short-beaked Common Dolphin;**
porpoising: Hugh Harrop.

p.76 **Short-beaked Common Dolphin;**
bow riding: Tim Olson.

p.77 **Short-beaked Common Dolphin;**
all images: Hugh Harrop.

p.79 **Bottlenose Dolphin;**
all images: Hugh Harrop.

p.80 **Bottlenose Dolphin;**
all images: Tim Stenton.

p.81 **Bottlenose Dolphin;**
all images: Tim Stenton.

p.83 **Risso's Dolphin;** *all images*: Hugh Harrop.

p.85 **Atlantic White-sided Dolphin;**
all images: Hugh Harrop.

p.87 **White-beaked Dolphin;** *all images*:
Chiara G Bertulli / Faxafloi Cetacean
Research.

p.89 **Harbour Porpoise;**
two animals together: Hilary Chambers.

p.89 **Harbour Porpoise;**
solitary animal: Tim Stenton.

CETACEANS – DEEPWATER SPECIES
p.90 All illustrations: Rob Still.
p.93 **Sei Whale;** *all images*: Alan Henry.
p.95 **Sperm Whale;** *blow*: Tim Stenton.
logging: Hugh Harrop.
Sperm Whale;
roll; fluke: Erwin Winkelman.

p.97 **Northern Bottlenose Whale;** *all images*:
Marina Milligan / Hal Whitehead Lab.

p.99 **Cuvier's beaked Whale;** *head and back*:
OCEANA / Juan Carlos Calvin.
Cuvier's beaked Whale;
scarred male: Hugh Harrop.
Cuvier's beaked Whale; *roll*: Tim Stenton.

p.101 **Sowerby's Beaked Whale;** *all images*:
Marina Milligan / Hal Whitehead Lab.

p.103 Beaked whale illustrations
– **see box below**: Rob Still.

p.105 **Striped Dolphin;** *all images*: Hugh Harrop.

CETACEANS – RARE SPECIES .
p.106 **True's beaked Whale:** Dylan Walker.
p.107 All illustrations: Rob Still.
p.108 **North Atlantic Right Whale;**
all images: Nicole Perkins.
p.109 **Blue Whale;** *roll; blow*: David Slater.
Blue Whale; *fluke*: Mike Baird.
p.111 **Dwarf Sperm Whale:** Glenn Overington.
p.111 **Pygmy Sperm Whale:** Bob Pitman.
p.112 **Beluga:** Hugh Harrop.
p.113 **Narwhal:** Todd Mintz.
p.114 **False Killer Whale:** Jim McLean.
p.115 **Melon-headed Whale:** Thomas Brown.
p.116 **Fraser's Dolphin:** Tim Stenton.
p.117 *Seal skinning*: Mary Bruce.
p.117 *Marine litter*: Andrew King.
p.118 *Killer Whale researchers in Shetland*:
Hugh Harrop.
p.118 **Killer Whale:** Hugh Harrop.
p.118 *Marine mammal rescue training*:
Stephen Marsh BDMLR.
p.120 *Seal watching*: Hugh Harrop
p.126 **Short-beaked Common Dolphin:**
Hugh Harrop

IMPORTANT NOTE

The lack of confirmed sightings of *Mesoplodon* beaked whales means that there is little reference material on which to base illustrations.

The illustrations throughout the book are based on limited photographic and video footage from the following sources:

True's Beaked Whale: Surface – Bay of Biscay (two encounters).

Gervais' Beaked Whale: Surface – Canary Islands. Strandings – Florida, Cayman Islands.

Sowerby's Beaked Whale: Surface – Bay of Biscay, Canary Islands. Underwater – Maldives. Strandings – Newfoundland, Scotland.

Blainville's Beaked Whale: Surface – Canary Islands. Underwater – Maldives. Stranding – North Carolina.

However, there may be a large variance in appearance, depending on factors such as location, age and gender. Notes relating to these variations are detailed alongside the illustrations.

Acknowledgments

The authors would like to say a special thank you to the following people for their invaluable help and assistance in this project: Chiara G Bertulli (Faxafloi Cetacean Research), Brian Clews (Wild*Guides*), Anne Donnelly (Shetland Wildlife), Paul Harvey (Shetland Biological Records Centre), Jim Irvine, John Lowrie Irvine (MV Zephyr), Tom and Cynthia Jamieson (formerly of Mousa Boat Trips), Stephen Marsh (BDMLR), Marina Milligan (Hal Whitehead Lab), Mary Ellen Odie, Patricia Odie, Glenn Overington (Shetland Wildlife); Nicole Perkins, Dr Helen Steward (Leeds University), Tim Stenton, Angeles Saez, Andy & Gill Swash (Wild*Guides*) Dylan Walker (Planet Whale) and Dr Jonathan Wills.

And to our respective families for their support over the past years and months: to Ethan and Paula; Anya, Rachel and Penny; and Cerys and Michelle – many thanks indeed.

Index

This index includes the common English and *scientific* names of all the sea mammals included in this book.

Common names in **bold** highlight the species that are afforded a full account.

Bold red numbers indicate the page number of the main species account.

Blue italicised numbers relate to other page(s) on which a photograph or illustration appears.

Normal black figures are used to indicate other key pages where the species is mentioned, but not illustrated.